Go Programming Language

by Wei-Meng Lee

A Wiley Brand

Go Programming Language For Dummies®

Published by: **John Wiley & Sons, Inc.,** 111 River Street, Hoboken, NJ 07030-5774, www.wiley.com

Copyright © 2021 by John Wiley & Sons, Inc., Hoboken, New Jersey

Published simultaneously in Canada

For general information on our other products and services, please contact our Customer Care Department within the U.S. at 877-762-2974, outside the U.S. at 317-572-3993, or fax 317-572-4002. For technical support, please visit https://hub.wiley.com/community/support/dummies.

Wiley publishes in a variety of print and electronic formats and by print-on-demand. Some material included with standard print versions of this book may not be included in e-books or in print-on-demand. If this book refers to media such as a CD or DVD that is not included in the version you purchased, you may download this material at http://booksupport.wiley.com. For more information about Wiley products, visit www.wiley.com.

Library of Congress Control Number: 2021934091

ISBN 978-1-119-78619-1 (pbk); ISBN 978-1-119-78620-7 (ebk); ISBN 978-1-119-78621-4 (ebk)

Manufactured in the United States of America

SKY10025829_032521

Contents at a Glance

Introduction 1

Part 1: Getting Started with Go 5
CHAPTER 1: Hello, Go! 7
CHAPTER 2: Working with Different Data Types 23
CHAPTER 3: Making Decisions 37
CHAPTER 4: Over and Over and Over: Using Loops 51
CHAPTER 5: Grouping Code into Functions 65

Part 2: Working with Data Structures 79
CHAPTER 6: Slicing and Dicing Using Arrays and Slices 81
CHAPTER 7: Defining the Blueprints of Your Data Using Structs 101
CHAPTER 8: Establishing Relationships Using Maps 113
CHAPTER 9: Encoding and Decoding Data Using JSON 129
CHAPTER 10: Defining Method Signatures Using Interfaces 151

Part 3: Multitasking in Go 163
CHAPTER 11: Threading Using Goroutines 165
CHAPTER 12: Communicating between Goroutines Using Channels 179

Part 4: Organizing Your Code 195
CHAPTER 13: Using and Creating Packages in Go 197
CHAPTER 14: Grouping Packages into Modules 211

Part 5: Seeing Go in Action 223
CHAPTER 15: Consuming Web APIs Using Go 225
CHAPTER 16: Getting Ready to Serve Using REST APIs 243
CHAPTER 17: Working with Databases 271

Part 6: The Part of Tens 285
CHAPTER 18: Ten Useful Go Packages to Create Applications 287
CHAPTER 19: Ten Great Go Resources 299

Index 303

Table of Contents

INTRODUCTION 1
 About This Book. 1
 Foolish Assumptions. 2
 Icons Used in This Book 2
 Beyond the Book 3
 Where to Go from Here 3

PART 1: GETTING STARTED WITH GO 5

CHAPTER 1: **Hello, Go!** 7
 Seeing What Learning Go Can Do for You 8
 Installing Go on Your Machine 9
  macOS 10
  Windows 11
 Using an Integrated Development Environment with Go 12
 Writing Your First Go Program 14
  Compiling and running the program 15
  Understanding how a Go program works 17
  Making sense of the Go file structure 18
  Compiling for multiple operating systems. 19
 Comparing Go with Other Languages 21
  Syntax 21
  Compilation 22
  Concurrency 22
  Library support 22

CHAPTER 2: **Working with Different Data Types** 23
 Declaring Always-Changing Variables. 24
  Using the var keyword: Type-inferred variables 24
  Specifying the data type: Explicitly typed variables 25
  Using the short variable declaration operator 26
 Declaring Never-Changing Constants. 27
 Removing Unused Variables 27
 Dealing with Strings 29
 Performing Type Conversions 30
  Discovering the type of a variable. 31
  Converting a variable's type. 32
  Interpolating strings 34

CHAPTER 3: **Making Decisions** 37
    Using If/Else Statements to Make Decisions 37
        Laying the foundation for the if/else statement:
        Logical and comparison operators 38
        Using the if/else statement 40
        Short-circuiting: Evaluating conditions in Go 42
    When You Have Too Many Conditions: Using the
    Switch Statement 46
        Switching with fall-throughs 47
        Matching multiple cases 48
        Switching without condition 48

CHAPTER 4: **Over and Over and Over: Using Loops** 51
    Performing Loops Using the for Statement 51
    Iterating over a Range of Values 56
        Iterating through arrays/slices 56
        Iterating through a string 58
    Using Labels with the for Loop 59

CHAPTER 5: **Grouping Code into Functions** 65
    Defining a Function 65
        Defining functions with parameters 66
        Defining functions with multiple parameters 68
        Passing arguments by value and by pointer 68
        Returning values from functions 71
        Naming return values 72
        Working with variadic functions 72
    Using Anonymous Functions 73
        Declaring an anonymous function 73
        Implementing closure using anonymous functions 74
        Implementing the filter() function using closure 76

PART 2: WORKING WITH DATA STRUCTURES 79
CHAPTER 6: **Slicing and Dicing Using Arrays and Slices** 81
    Arming Yourself to Use Arrays 81
        Declaring an array 82
        Initializing an array 83
        Working with multidimensional arrays 83
    Sleuthing Out the Secrets of Slices 86
        Creating an empty slice 86
        Creating and initializing a slice 88
        Appending to a slice 88
    Slicing and Ranging 92
        Extracting part of an array or slice 92
        Iterating through a slice 95

Making copies of an array or slice. 95
Inserting an item into a slice 97
Removing an item from a slice 99

CHAPTER 7: **Defining the Blueprints of Your Data
Using Structs** 101
Defining Structs for a Collection of Items 101
Creating a Go Struct 104
Making a Copy of a Struct 105
Defining Methods in Structs 107
Comparing Structs. 110

CHAPTER 8: **Establishing Relationships Using Maps**. 113
Creating Maps in Go 113
Initializing a map with a map literal 115
Checking the existence of a key 115
Deleting a key. 116
Getting the number of items in a map. 116
Iterating over a map 117
Getting all the keys in a map 117
Setting the iteration order in a map. 118
Sorting the items in a map by values 118
Using Structs and Maps in Go 121
Creating a map of structs. 121
Sorting a map of structs 124

CHAPTER 9: **Encoding and Decoding Data Using JSON** 129
Getting Acquainted with JSON. 129
Object 130
String. 130
Boolean. 131
Number. 131
Object 132
Array 132
null. 133
Decoding JSON. 134
Decoding JSON to a struct 135
Decoding JSON to arrays 136
Decoding embedded objects. 137
Mapping custom attribute names. 140
Mapping unstructured data. 141
Encoding JSON 144
Encoding structs to JSON 144
Encoding interfaces to JSON 148

CHAPTER 10: **Defining Method Signatures Using Interfaces**.....151

Working with Interfaces in Go...................................152
Defining an interface..152
Implementing an interface.....................................153
Looking at How You May Use Interfaces......................154
Adding methods to a type that doesn't satisfy an interface.....158
Using the Stringer interface..................................159
Implementing multiple interfaces.............................160
Using an empty interface......................................161
Determining whether a value implements a specific interface ...162

PART 3: MULTITASKING IN GO 163

CHAPTER 11: **Threading Using Goroutines**........................165

Understanding Goroutines 166
Using Goroutines with Shared Resources.....................168
Seeing how shared resources impact goroutines 168
Accessing shared resources using mutual exclusion........171
Using atomic counters for modifying shared resources 172
Synchronizing Goroutines 174

CHAPTER 12: **Communicating between Goroutines
Using Channels**...179

Understanding Channels 179
How channels work...180
How channels are used 183
Iterating through Channels 186
Asynchronously Waiting on Channels 187
Using Buffered Channels 192

PART 4: ORGANIZING YOUR CODE..........................195

CHAPTER 13: **Using and Creating Packages in Go**................197

Working with Packages...197
Creating shareable packages..................................200
Organizing packages using directories........................202
Using Third-Party Packages 204
Emojis for Go 204
Go Documentation 205

CHAPTER 14: **Grouping Packages into Modules**...................211

Creating a Module...211
Testing and Building a Module 214
Publishing a Module on GitHub 216

PART 5: SEEING GO IN ACTION 223

CHAPTER 15: **Consuming Web APIs Using Go** 225
    Understanding Web APIs 225
    Fetching Data from Web Services in Go. 226
        Writing a Go program to connect to a web API. 227
        Decoding JSON data 229
        Refactoring the code for decoding JSON data. 233
        Fetching from multiple web services at the same time. 238
        Returning Goroutine's results to the main() function 239

CHAPTER 16: **Getting Ready to Serve Using REST APIs** 243
    Building Web Services Using REST APIs 243
        HTTP messages 244
        REST URLs. 244
        REST methods 246
        REST response 248
    Creating a REST API in Go. 249
        Getting your REST API up and running. .249
        Testing the REST API 251
        Registering additional paths 251
        Passing in query string 254
        Specifying request methods 255
        Storing the course information on the REST API 257
        Testing the REST API again. 267

CHAPTER 17: **Working with Databases** 271
    Setting Up a MySQL Database Server. 272
        Interfacing with the MySQL server 272
        Creating a database and table. 274
        Creating a new account and granting permission 275
    Connecting to the MySQL Database in Go. .276
        Retrieving a record 278
        Adding a record 280
        Modifying a record 281
        Deleting a record. 283

PART 6: THE PART OF TENS. 285

CHAPTER 18: **Ten Useful Go Packages to Create Applications**. . .287
    color. 287
        Installation 288
        Code sample. 288
    now 288
        Installation 288
        Code sample. 288

go-pushbullet 289
        Installation 289
        Code sample. 289
goid 290
        Installation 290
        Code sample. 290
json2go 291
        Installation 291
        Code sample. 291
gojq 292
        Installation 293
        Code sample. 293
turtle 294
        Installation 294
        Code sample. 294
go-http-client 295
        Installation 295
        Code sample. 295
notify 296
        Installation 296
        Code sample. 296
gosx-notifier 297
        Installation 297
        Code sample. 297

CHAPTER 19: **Ten Great Go Resources** 299
    The Official Go Website 299
    Go by Example. 300
    A Tour of Go 300
    The Go Frequently Asked Questions 300
    The Go Playground 300
    Go Bootcamp. 301
    Effective Go 301
    Gophercises 301
    Tutorialspoint. 301
    Stack Overflow 302

INDEX 303

Introduction

Today, if you're a programmer, you have lots of options when it comes to choosing a programming language. Popular programming languages include C++, C#, Go, Java, JavaScript, Python, R, Swift, and many more. Each language is designed to solve a different set of problems and, depending on what you're going to create (mobile apps, web apps, desktop apps), you may end up learning one or more of these languages.

So, why Go? Turns out that three engineers at Google were frustrated with the various toolsets that they were working on and set out to design a new language that would address the criticisms of other languages while at the same time keeping their useful features.

Go was designed to

>> Use static typing and have the run-time efficiency of C

>> Have the readability and usability of languages like Python and JavaScript

>> Exhibit great performance in networking and multiprocessing

The problems with existing languages forced the team at Google to design a new language from the ground up, creating a lean and mean language designed for massive multithreading and concurrency.

This book covers the basics of Go (also known as Golang), one of the fastest-growing programming languages specifically designed to build faster and more scalable applications.

About This Book

In this code-intensive book, you're encouraged to try out the various examples, which are designed to be compact, easy to follow, and easy to understand. But you don't have to read the book from the first page to the last. Each chapter is designed to be independent, so you can dive in wherever you want and find the topics that you want to start learning.

If you're short on time, you can safely skip sidebars (text in gray boxes) or anything marked with the Technical Stuff icon (more on that in "Icons Used in This Book," later in this Introduction). They're interesting, but they aren't essential to understanding the subject at hand.

Within this book, you may note that some web addresses break across two lines of text. If you're reading this book in print and want to visit one of these web pages, simply key in the web address exactly as it's noted in the text, pretending as though the line break doesn't exist. If you're reading this as an e-book, you've got it easy — just click the web address to be taken directly to the web page.

Foolish Assumptions

This book is for people who are new (or relatively new) to Go. I don't assume that you're familiar with Go programming, but I do assume the following:

>> You're familiar with the basics of programming.

>> You're familiar with the concept of data structures, such as dictionary, arrays, and structs.

>> You have a computer that you can use to try out the examples in this book.

Icons Used in This Book

Like other books in the *For Dummies* series, this book uses icons, little pictures in the margin to draw your attention to certain kinds of material. Here are the icons that I use:

REMEMBER

Whenever I tell you something useful or important enough that you'd do well to store the information somewhere safe in your memory for later recall, I flag it with the Remember icon.

TECHNICAL STUFF

The Technical Stuff icon marks text that contains some for-nerds-only technical details or explanations that you're free to skip.

TIP

The Tip icon marks shortcuts or easier ways to do things, which I hope will make your life easier.

WARNING

The Warning icon marks text that contains a friendly but unusually insistent reminder to avoid doing something. You've been warned.

Beyond the Book

In addition to what you're reading right now, this product comes with a free access-anywhere Cheat Sheet that tells you how to try Go online without installing any additional software, how to use the online tools to convert JSON to Go structs, and how to use Go in Docker. To get this Cheat Sheet, go to www.dummies. com and type **Go Programming Language For Dummies Cheat Sheet** in the Search box.

This book includes some downloadable content as well. Go to www.dummies.com/go/goprogramminglanguagefd to download all the code in the book.

Where to Go from Here

If you're totally new to Go, you may want to start from the first chapter and follow through to the end. If you already have some basic knowledge of Go, you may want to head to Part 5, where you see Go in action. Regardless of how much experience you have, you can always turn to the index or table of contents to find the subjects that interest you most.

Finally, my advice to all beginners is: Practice, practice, practice. Type in the code in each chapter and make mistakes. The more mistakes you make, the better you'll understand and remember the topics discussed.

Good luck and enjoy your newfound knowledge!

1

Getting Started with Go

IN THIS PART . . .

Write your first Go program.

Discover the basic data types in Go and find out how to declare variables and constants.

Explore the various logical and comparison operators and use them to make decisions.

Understand how looping works and how you can execute code repeatedly.

Use functions to create Go programs that are easy to maintain and understand.

Chapter **1**

Hello, Go!

G o is an open-source programming language — one of the fastest-growing programming languages around — released by Google in 2009. It's a multipurpose programming language specifically designed to build fast, scalable applications.

TECHNICAL STUFF

Go comes from a pretty impressive team of people: Ken Thompson (designer and creator of Unix and C), Rob Pike (cocreator of UTF-8 and Unix format), and Robert Griesemer (a Google engineer). If you're technically inclined, you may want to check out an article called "Go at Google: Language Design in the Service of Software Engineering" (https://talks.golang.org/2012/splash.article), which discusses how Go was initially conceived to solve problems at Google.

In this chapter, I explain why learning Go is important for your career, where Go can be used, and how to get started with Go programming.

TIP

Go is often referred to as Golang because of its web address: https://golang.org. However, the official name of the language is Go, so that's how I refer to it throughout this book.

Seeing What Learning Go Can Do for You

You can learn many programming languages today, but Go stands out from the others for a few reasons:

>> **Go is easy to learn.** Go's syntax makes it a readable language. It has no support for object-oriented programming (OOP), which means you don't have to worry about classes and inheritance and the complexities that come with that.

TECHNICAL STUFF

Object-oriented programming (OOP) is a programming paradigm that is based on the concept of *objects* (data). Instead of focusing on the functions and logics, OOP organizes software around data, or objects. A key concept in OOP is *classes* (sort of like templates). Suppose you want to display buttons in your application. Instead of writing the code to display each button individually, you can create a class to represent a generic button and use it to create buttons to display in your application. Each button has its own *properties* (characteristics). Using the concept of *inheritance* in OOP, you can create multiple *subclasses* of the button class to create different types of buttons, such as a rounded button, a rectangular button, and so on.

>> **Go has fewer features than other programming languages.** You don't have to worry about the best way to solve a problem — there is only one right way to solve a problem in Go. This makes your codebase easy to maintain.

>> **Go excels in concurrent programming.** Go's support for *Goroutines* makes it extremely easy to run multiple functions concurrently.

TIP

Go has no support for *generics* (the ability to specify the actual data type until it's actually used), but this may change as the language evolves.

If you still aren't convinced that you should learn Go, perhaps this next bit of news will motivate you: In the Stack Overflow Developer Survey 2019 (https://insights.stackoverflow.com/survey/2019), Go developers were the third highest paid in the industry, behind Clojure and F# developers.

Although Go has been around for quite a while (since 2009), only recently did it get wide adoption by developers, thanks to the proliferation of cloud computing and microservices. Today, Go has been widely used by major companies such as Dailymotion, Dropbox, Google, and Uber.

Here are some examples of where Go can be used:

>> **Cloud services:** You can build scalable apps using Go on the Google Cloud Platform (GCP).

- » **Networking apps:** With Go's support for Goroutines, you can use Go to build distributed servers and application programming interfaces (APIs).

- » **Web services:** You can use Go to build scalable and efficient web services.

- » **Command-line apps:** Because Go runs on multiple platforms, you can compile the same codebase and target different platforms (such as those running on macOS and Windows).

Installing Go on Your Machine

You're probably very eager to get started with Go programming on your machine, so let's get to it!

The easiest way to install Go is to go to `https://golang.org/doc/install`. This website automatically detects the operating system (OS) you're using and shows you the button to click to download the Go installer (see Figure 1-1).

FIGURE 1-1:
Downloading the
Go installer.

TIP

This book code has been written and tested using Go version 1.15. When you're reading this book, a new version of Go may have been released. In order to ensure that you can follow the examples in this book, I strongly suggest that you install the same version of Go that I've used. You can find it here:

>> **macOS:** https://golang.org/dl/go1.15.8.darwin-amd64.pkg

>> **Windows:** https://golang.org/dl/go1.15.8.windows-amd64.msi

TECHNICAL
STUFF

If you want to be able to choose the Go installer for each of the supported operating systems (Linux, macOS, and Windows), and even see the source code for Go, go to https://golang.org/dl/.

After you've downloaded the Go installer, double-click the installer to start the straightforward installation process. I recommend that you just use the default installation settings — you don't need to change any of those settings.

In the following sections, I show you how to verify that your installation is performed successfully on macOS and Windows.

macOS

On macOS, the Go installer installs the Go distribution in the /usr/local/go directory. It also adds the /usr/local/go/bin directory to your PATH environment variable. You can verify this by entering the following command in the Terminal app (which you can find in the Applications/Utilities folder):

```
$ echo $PATH
```

You should see something like the following output (note the added path, highlighted in bold):

```
/Users/weimenglee/opt/anaconda3/bin:/Volumes/SSD/opt/anaco
nda3/condabin:/Users/weimenglee/flutter/bin:/Users/weimeng
lee/go/bin:/Users/weimenglee/.nvm/versions/node/v9.2.0/bin
:/usr/local/bin:/usr/bin:/bin:/usr/sbin:/sbin:/usr/local/g
o/bin:/usr/local/share/dotnet:~/.dotnet/tools:/Library/App
le/usr/bin:/Library/Frameworks/Mono.framework/Versions/Cur
rent/Commands
```

TIP

Make sure to restart the Terminal app after you've installed Go in order for the changes to take effect.

To verify that the installation is correct, type the following command in Terminal:

```
$ go version
```

You should see the version of Go installed on your system:

```
go version go1.15.8 darwin/amd64
```

Windows

On Windows, the Go installer installs the Go distribution in the C:\Go directory. It also adds the C:\Go\bin directory to your PATH environment variable. You can verify this by entering the following command in Command Prompt (which you can find by typing **cmd** in the Windows search box):

```
C:\Users\Wei-Meng Lee>path
```

You should see something like the following output (note the added path, high-lighted in bold):

```
PATH=C:\WINDOWS\system32;C:\WINDOWS;C:\WINDOWS\System32\
Wbem;C:\WINDOWS\System32\WindowsPowerShell\v1.0\;C:\WIND
OWS\System32\OpenSSH\;C:\Program Files\dotnet\;C:\Program
Files\Microsoft SQL Server\130\Tools\Binn\;C:\Go\bin;
C:\Program Files\Git\cmd;C:\Program Files\Graphviz
 2.44.1\bin;C:\Program Files\CMake\bin;C:\Program
Files\Docker\Docker\resources\bin;C:\ProgramData\DockerDes
ktop\version-bin;C:\Program Files\MySQL\MySQL Shell
8.0\bin\;C:\Users\Wei-Meng Lee\AppData\Local\
Microsoft\WindowsApps;;C:\Users\Wei-Meng Lee\
AppData\Local\Programs\Microsoft VS Code\bin;C:\Users\Wei-
Meng Lee\.dotnet\tools;C:\Users\Wei-Meng Lee\go\bin
```

TIP

Make sure to restart the Command Prompt window after you've installed Go in order for the changes to take effect.

To verify that the installation is correct, type the following command in Command Prompt:

```
C:\Users\Wei-Meng Lee>go version
```

You should now see the version of Go installed on your computer:

```
go version go1.15.8 windows/amd64
```

Using an Integrated Development Environment with Go

To develop applications using Go, you just need a text editor (such as Visual Studio Code, TextEdit on macOS, or even the old trusty NotePad), and you're good to go (pun unintended). However, many developers prefer to use integrated development environments (IDEs) that can help them organize their code, as well as provide debugging support. Here is a partial list of IDEs that work with Go:

» **Visual Studio Code** (https://code.visualstudio.com): Visual Studio Code from Microsoft is the mother of all code editors (and my personal favorite). Visual Studio Code is a full-featured code editor that supports almost all programming languages under the sun. Perhaps one of the most useful features of Visual Studio Code is IntelliSense, which helps to complete your statement as you type. It also comes with debugger support and an interactive console, as well as Git integration. Best of all, Visual Studio Code is free and has a very active community of Go developers, allowing you to extend its functionalities through the various plug-ins.

» **GoLand** (www.jetbrains.com/go/): GoLand is a cross-platform IDE by JetBrains. It comes with coding assistance, a debugger, an integrated Terminal, and more. GoLand is a commercial IDE, and it has a 30-day trial.

» **The Go Playground** (https://play.golang.org): The Go Playground (which isn't really an IDE, but is worth a mention here) is a web service that runs on Go's servers. It receives a Go program, compiles, links, runs it inside a sandbox, and then returns the output. The Go Playground is very useful when you need to test out some Go code quickly using a web browser.

TIP

In this book, I use Visual Studio Code for Go development. To download Visual Studio Code, go to https://code.visualstudio.com/download. After you've downloaded and installed Visual Studio Code, launch it, and you should see the screen shown in Figure 1-2.

TIP

In order for Visual Studio Code to recognize your Go language syntax, you also need to install an extension for it. Follow these steps to install the Go extension:

1. In Visual Studio Code, click the Extensions icon on the Activity Bar (see Figure 1-3).

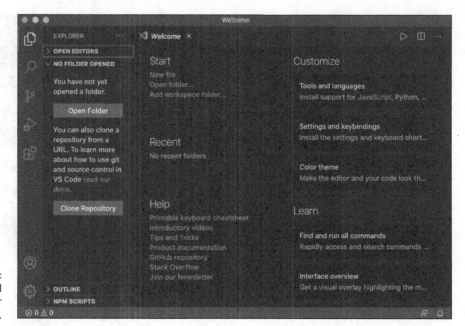

FIGURE 1-2:
Launching Visual
Studio Code for
the first time.

FIGURE 1-3:
The Extensions
icon is located at
the bottom of the
Activity Bar.

2. **In the Search box for the Extensions panel, type** Go.

   You see a list of the Go extensions available (see Figure 1-4).

3. **Select the first extension and click the Install button on the right.**

   That's it! You're ready to write your first program!

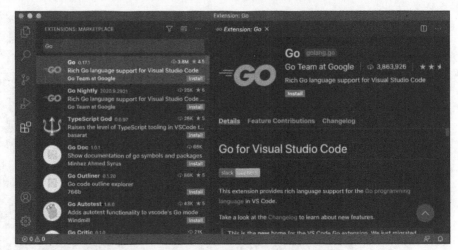

FIGURE 1-4:
Searching for
Go extensions
for Visual
Studio Code.

Writing Your First Go Program

To write your first Go program, create a new file in Visual Studio Code by choosing File ⇨ New File. Then enter the following statements (see Figure 1-5):

```go
package main

import "fmt"

func main() {
    fmt.Println("Hello, world!")
}
```

FIGURE 1-5:
Writing your first
Go program.

When you're done typing, press ⌘+S (Ctrl+S) to save the file. Name the file main.go. If this is the first time you're writing a Go program using Visual Studio Code, it may prompt you to download additional plugins for Go. I recommend that you install the plugins.

TIP

For this book, save your files to a folder named with the chapter number you're reading. For example, save main.go in a folder named Chapter 1 in your home directory. On a Mac, that looks like this:

```
~/Chapter 1
    |__main.go
```

In Windows, it looks like this:

```
C:\users\yourname\Chapter 1
    |__main.go
```

After the file is saved, notice that your Go statements will now be color-coded — light blue for keywords such as package, import, and func; orange for strings like Hello, world! and fmt; and yellow for functions like main() and Println().

Compiling and running the program

After you've saved a program, you need to compile it so that you can run it.

You can run the program directly in Visual Studio Code. To do that, launch the Terminal by choosing Terminal⇨New Terminal. The Terminal now opens in Visual Studio Code (see Figure 1-6).

Next, change the directory to Chapter 1. In macOS, use the following command:

```
$ cd ~/"Chapter 1"
```

In Windows, use the following command:

```
$ cd "C:\users\username\Chapter 1"
```

To compile the main.go file, type the following command:

```
$ go build main.go
```

FIGURE 1-6:
You can directly access the Terminal in Visual Studio Code.

The preceding command compiles the main.go program into an executable file. On macOS, after running the program, you see a file named main. To run it, use the following command:

```
$ ./main
Hello, world!
```

If you see the Hello, world! string printed, congratulations! You're now officially a Go programmer!

If you're using Windows, the build command generates an executable named main.exe. To run it, use the following command:

```
C:\users\username\Chapter 1>main
Hello, world!
```

Because you often want to run the program immediately after compiling it, you can use the run option to compile and run the program straight away:

```
$ go run main.go
```

Understanding how a Go program works

Now that your Go program works, it's time to understand how. I'll walk you through it line by line. The first line defines the package name for this program:

```
package main
```

Go programs are organized into *packages*. A package is a collection of source files grouped in a single directory. In this example, main is the name of the package stored in the Chapter 1 directory. If you have additional source files (.go files), they'll all belong to this main package (more on this in later chapters).

TIP

You aren't constrained to using main as the package name. You can use any package name you want. But this main package name has a special meaning: Packages with the name main will contain a function named main(), which serves as an entry point for your program to get started. Also, your package name and the name of the file containing it don't need to be the same. I could've named the file dog.go instead of main.go, and the program would still run (but now the executable would be named dog instead of main).

The next line imports a package named fmt:

```
import "fmt"
```

This package contains various functions to allow you to format and print to the console. It also contains functions to get a user's inputs.

TIP

If you're new to programming, a function is a block of code that's used to perform a single, related task. Turn to Chapter 5 for more about functions.

The next block of code is the main entry point of your program:

```
func main() {

}
```

Because the package name is main, this main() function will now serve as the starting point for your program to execute.

Finally, the following line calls the Println() function from the fmt package to print the string Hello, world! to the console:

```
fmt.Println("Hello, world!")
```

Making sense of the Go file structure

You should now have a good idea of how the Go program works. Let's dive a little deeper into how Go files are grouped together. As I mention in the previous section, all files in the same directory belong to the same package. So, let's now add another file to the Chapter 1 directory and name it show_time.go. The Chapter 1 directory should now have one more file:

```
Chapter 1
    |__main.go
    |__show_time.go
```

Populate the show_time.go file with the following statements:

```
package main

import (
    "fmt"
    "time"
)

func displayTime() {
    fmt.Println(time.Now())
}
```

Notice that the file is part of the main package (the first line reflects that). Also, you can import multiple packages by enclosing them within a pair of parentheses. In this case, we imported the time package in addition to the fmt package. Finally, we also added a function named displayTime(), which displays the current date and time using the Now() function from the time package.

Because the displayTime() function belongs to the main package, it can also be called from main.go:

```
package main

import "fmt"

func main() {
    fmt.Println("Hello, world!")
    displayTime()
}
```

TIP

You can call functions defined in the same package without needing to import the package.

Because there are now two files in the package (`main`), you don't build the program using a specific filename. Instead, you just need to use the `build` command within the `Chapter 1` directory:

```
$ go build
```

This time around, you'll see that there is a new file named `Chapter_1` (in Windows, you'll see a file named `Chapter_1.exe`) created in the `Chapter 1` directory.

To run it in macOS, type the following in Terminal:

```
$ ./Chapter_1
```

To run it in Windows, type the following command:

```
C:\users\username\Chapter 1>Chapter_1
```

You should now be able to see the output:

```
Hello, world!
2020-10-01 12:01:13.412568 +0800 +08 m=+0.000365532
```

Compiling for multiple operating systems

When you install Go, the Go installer automatically sets up a number of Go environment variables in order for your Go program to work correctly. Specifically, it auto-detects values of the host architecture and OS and sets the GOHOSTARCH and GOHOSTOS environment variables, respectively. The value of these two variables will be used as the target platform for your program to compile to.

To examine the values of these Go environment variables, use the `env` command:

```
$ go env
GOARCH="amd64"
GOBIN=""
GOCACHE="/Users/weimenglee/Library/Caches/go-build"
GOEXE=""
GOFLAGS=""
GOHOSTARCH="amd64"
```

```
GOHOSTOS="darwin"
GOOS="darwin"
...

...
PKG_CONFIG="pkg-config"
```

To compile your program for another OS, you need to set another two environment variables: GOOS and GOARCH. These two variables configure the target OS based on the values shown in Table 1-1.

TABLE 1-1

Environment Variables for the Various Operating Systems

Operating Systems	GOOS	GOARCH
macOS	darwin	amd64
Linux	linux	amd64
Windows	windows	amd64

To compile for macOS, use the following command and options:

```
$ GOOS=darwin GOARCH=amd64 go build -o Chapter_1-mac
```

TIP

In the near future, when Go has been ported natively to Apple Silicon, the value of GOARCH would be arm64.

To compile for the Windows OS, use the following command and options:

```
$ cd ~/"Chapter 1"
$ GOOS=windows GOARCH=amd64 go build -o Chapter_1-windows.exe
```

TIP

The -o option (short for *output*) allows you to specify the name of the executable file.

The preceding command compiles the package in the Chapter 1 folder to run on Windows and save the executable as Chapter_1-windows.exe.

To compile for Linux, use the following command and options:

```
$ GOOS=linux GOARCH=amd64 go build -o Chapter_1-linux
```

TIP

If you use Go on the Raspberry Pi, then you should specify arm64 for GOARCH.

If you're running macOS or Linux, you can use the `file` command to examine the various executables created for each platform:

```
$ file Chapter_1-mac
Chapter_1-mac: Mach-O 64-bit executable x86_64

$ file Chapter_1-windows.exe
Chapter_1-windows.exe: PE32+ executable (console) x86-64
    (stripped to external PDB), for MS Windows

$ file Chapter_1-linux
Chapter_1-linux: ELF 64-bit LSB executable, x86-64, version 1
    (SYSV), statically linked, Go BuildID=bSETwZgNDR5vlulRHnzw/
    KNpENRt9Hipd8Nu7HGDg/v38ZPzDs35yMw33hUxoz/Y_cNfU8fID2cCtz36hCq,
    not stripped
```

Comparing Go with Other Languages

When learning a new programming language, it's always helpful to try to compare it with another language that you may already be familiar with. Doing so allows you to try to map your current knowledge to the new language that you're trying to learn.

In this section, I compare Go with two of the most commonly used programming languages used in the industry, Java and Python. Occasionally, I compare Go with C, because Go is syntactically similar to C. Go is often touted as the language with the speed of C and the productivity of Python.

REMEMBER

If you aren't familiar with any of the languages listed in this section, don't worry! In this book, I cover all the features mentioned here.

Syntax

In terms of syntax, Go is closer to C and Java, which use curly braces to enclose blocks of code. This syntax differs from Python, which uses indentation as a form of denoting blocks of code.

Like Python, Go functions are first-class citizens, whereas in Java everything revolves around classes, and you need a class just to enclose a function.

Unlike Python and Java, Go doesn't have OOP support, and it doesn't support inheritance. But it does have interfaces and structs that work just like classes.

Go is statically typed, like Java. It differs from Python, which is dynamically typed.

Compilation

Whereas Python and Java are compiled to byte code, which is then interpreted and run on a virtual machine, Go compiles directly to machine code, which makes Go take the lead in terms of performance.

Like Python and Java, Go is also garbage collected. In programming, garbage collection (GC) is a form of automatic memory management. The garbage collector tries to reclaim memory occupied by objects that are no longer in use by the program.

Python is extremely memory intensive. Java is not much better because everything is heap allocated. But Go affords more control of memory usage.

Concurrency

Go has parallelism and concurrency built in, which means writing multi-threaded applications is very easy. Both Java and Python support concurrency through threading, but they aren't as efficient as Go. In fact, concurrency is one of Go's main selling points.

Library support

All three languages have huge library support — both standard and third-party libraries. A language's survival depends in large part on its support for third-party libraries. That's why Python has been so hot for the past couple of years — its support for third-party libraries for doing data analytics brings machine learning and deep learning readily to the masses. Although Go doesn't have the scale of third-party library support that Python does because it's young, the number of libraries for Go is growing.

IN THIS CHAPTER

» **Declaring variables**

» **Declaring constants**

» **Getting rid of unused variables**

» **Manipulating strings**

» **Converting the data type of one value to another**

Chapter **2**

Working with Different Data Types

This chapter explores one of the foundational building blocks of programming: how to declare variables and constants in Go. This chapter also tells you how to manipulate strings in Go and how to convert data from one type to another.

REMEMBER

In Go, there are four types of data:

» **Basic:** Examples include strings, numbers, and Booleans.

» **Aggregate:** Examples include arrays and structs.

» **Reference:** Examples include pointers, slices, functions, and channels.

» **Interface:** An interface is a collection of method signatures.

In this chapter, I focus on the basic data types in Go. (I cover the other data types throughout the rest of this book.)

Declaring Always-Changing Variables

In programming, variables are containers that store values. These values may change over the lifetime of the program. In Go, you can declare and initialize variables in a variety of ways. I cover the possibilities in the following sections.

Using the var keyword: Type-inferred variables

The first way to declare a variable is to prefix the variable name with the var keyword and then assign it a value, as in the following example:

```
package main

import "fmt"

func main() {
    var num1 = 5            // type inferred
    fmt.Println(num1)       // 5
}
```

TIP

In Go, anything that follows the double-slash (//) is a comment. The compiler will ignore your comments, but adding comments to your code is usually a good practice because it makes it more understandable.

In the preceding example, num1 is a variable whose type is an integer. Because it's assigned the value of 5 during declaration, its type is inferred to be that of int (integer).

REMEMBER

In Go, a compilation error occurs if you declare a variable but you don't make use of it (for example, by printing its value). So, in the previous example, one way to resolve this issue is to print it out using the Println() function. If you don't resolve the issue, your program won't compile.

A variable can be defined outside a function as well, as the following example shows:

```
package main

import "fmt"
```

```
var num1 = 5              // type inferred

func main() {
    fmt.Println(num1) // 5
}
```

Variables that are defined outside functions are accessible to all functions.

Specifying the data type: Explicitly typed variables

You can specify the data type of the variable explicitly when declaring them, as the following example demonstrates:

```
package main

import "fmt"

func main() {
    var num1 = 5              // type inferred
    var num2 int              // explicitly typed

    fmt.Println(num1)
    fmt.Println(num2)
}
```

Here, num2 is explicitly declared to be an int variable. When you print out its value, you see 0. Variables declared without initialization are given their *zero value*. The zero values for the various types are shown below:

```
var num3 float32     // floating point variable
var name string      // string variable
var raining bool     // boolean variable

fmt.Println(num3)    // 0
fmt.Println(name)    // "" (empty string)
fmt.Println(raining) // false
```

You can also explicitly declare and initialize a value at the same time, like this:

```
var rates float32 = 4.5  // declared as float32 and
                         // then initialized
```

Using the short variable declaration operator

Another way to declare and initialize a variable is to use the *short variable declaration operator* (:=), like this:

```
firstName := "Wei-Meng"
```

Here, I'm declaring `firstName` as a `string` variable by initializing it to the string `"Wei-Meng"`, all without needing to use the `var` prefix.

You can also declare and initialize multiple variables (of different types) in a single statement, like this:

```
firstName, lastName, age := "Wei-Meng", "Lee", 25
```

This method also works with the `var` keyword:

```
var firstName, lastName string = "Wei-Meng", "Lee"
```

Note that if you're declaring and initializing multiple variables using the `var` keyword, all the variables must be of the same type. The following is not allowed:

```
var firstName, lastName string, age int = "Wei-Meng",
    "Lee", 25
```

The preceding statement can be fixed by removing the data type, like this:

```
var firstName, lastName, age = "Wei-Meng", "Lee", 25
```

Alternatively, you can declare them this way:

```
var (
    firstName string = "Wei-Meng"
    lastName  string = "Lee"
    age       int    = 25
)
```

When you declare and initialize a variable using the := operator, you can't use it for variables declared outside function bodies, like the following:

```
import (
    "fmt"
)
```

```
num1 := 5    // error; non-declaration statement
             // outside function body

func main() {

    fmt.Println("Hello, world!")
}
```

REMEMBER

The := operator can only be used for declaring and initializing variables inside functions.

Declaring Never-Changing Constants

Like variables, constants are containers. But unlike variables, the value of a constant, after it's initialized, will never change.

You define constants the way you define variables in Go, except that you fix the statement using the const keyword instead of the var keyword, like this:

```
package main

import "fmt"

const publisher = "Wiley"

func main() {
    fmt.Println(publisher)
}
```

TIP

A const can appear anywhere a var statement can.

Removing Unused Variables

If you've ever programmed before, you're all too familiar with this situation: You declare some variables, but you don't use them in your program. Consider the following:

```
package main

import (
```

```
        "fmt"
)

func main() {
    var num1 = 5
    fmt.Println("Hello, world!")
}
```

Notice that num1 is declared and initialized a value. However, I didn't use it anywhere in the program. If you do this, the Go compiler will flag an error (num1 declared and not used) when you try to run it. According to the Go FAQ:

> The presence of an unused variable may indicate a bug, while unused imports just slow down compilation. Accumulate enough unused imports in your code tree and things can get very slow. For these reasons, Go allows neither.

Also, if you import a package and you don't use it, the compiler similarly raises an error. Interestingly, if a variable is declared outside a function and not used anywhere in the program, like the following, the compiler wouldn't complain:

```
package main

import (
    "fmt"
)

var num1 = 5

func main() {
    fmt.Println("Hello, world!")
}
```

For variables declared inside function bodies, you need to use them, or else you'll get an error message.

REMEMBER

If you insist on having unused variables in your program, Go offers a quick way to address this issue. Simply assign the unused variable to a blank identifier (_), like this:

TIP

```
var num1 = 5
_ = num1   // The compiler is now happy!
```

Dealing with Strings

In Go, a string is a read-only slice of bytes. Think of string as a collection of bytes. (I explain slices in more detail in Chapter 6.)

The earlier example shows one example of strings in Go:

```
firstName string = "Wei-Meng"
```

A string can contain special characters (such as \n or \t), as shown in the following example:

```
address := "The White House\n1600 Pennsylvania Avenue
NW\nWashington, DC 20500"
```

When the address variable is printed with the Println() function, the output looks like this:

```
The White House
1600 Pennsylvania Avenue NW
Washington, DC 20500
```

Go also supports raw strings. A raw string is enclosed by a pair of back ticks (``). It can span multiple lines, and special characters have no meaning in it. Here's an example of a raw string:

```
quotation := `"Anyone who has never made
a mistake has never tried
anything new."
--Albert Einstein`

fmt.Println(quotation)
```

The output of the preceding block of code is:

```
"Anyone who has never made
a mistake has never tried
anything new."
--Albert Einstein
```

You can also represent Unicode characters in your strings, as the following examples illustrate:

```
str1 := "你好,世界"        // Chinese
str2 := "こんにちは世界"     // Japanese
```

Instead of Unicode characters, you can also use the Unicode encodings of each character in your strings:

```
str3 := "\u4f60\u597d\uff0c\u4e16\u754c" // 你好,世界
```

TIP

You can try your hand at converting Chinese characters to their Unicode representations at www.chineseconverter.com/en/convert/unicode.

Each Chinese or Japanese character takes up 3 bytes, so if you use the len() function on the string variables, you get the following results:

```
fmt.Println(len(str1))  // 15 = 5 chars * 3 bytes
fmt.Println(len(str2))  // 21 = 7 chars * 3 bytes
fmt.Println(len(str3))  // 15 = 5 chars * 3 bytes
```

If you want to count the number of characters (runes) in a string, use the RuneCountInString() function:

```
fmt.Println(utf8.RuneCountInString(str1)) // 5
fmt.Println(utf8.RuneCountInString(str2)) // 7
fmt.Println(utf8.RuneCountInString(str3)) // 5
```

TECHNICAL STUFF

A *rune* is any of the characters of certain ancient alphabets (for example, a script used for writing the Germanic languages).

Performing Type Conversions

In programming, type conversion happens when you want to convert the data type of one value into another. For example, you may have a string that contains a numeric value "45". However, because this value is represented as a string, you can't perform any mathematical operations on it. You need to explicitly convert this string type into an integer type before you can perform any mathematical operations on it.

Due to the strong type system in Go, you need to perform all type conversions explicitly yourself. In other languages, type conversion is usually referred to as *type casting*, but in Go, the official name for this is *type conversion*.

Before you can understand how to perform type conversion, you need to understand how to discover the type of a variable.

Discovering the type of a variable

You can use type inferencing when creating your variables (see "Using the `var` keyword: Type-inferred variables," earlier in this chapter). And because of this, you sometimes want (or need) to know the data type of a particular variable. Consider the following statement:

```
firstName, lastName, age := "Wei-Meng", "Lee", 25
```

In the preceding statement, you can easily guess the data types of `firstName` (string), `lastName` (string), and `age` (int). However, suppose you have the following statement:

```
start := time.Now()  // need to import the time package
```

What is the data type of `start`? It's not so obvious. There are two methods for finding out the data type of a variable:

» **Use the `%T` printing verb in the `Printf()` function.** It looks like this:

```
fmt.Printf("%T\n", start)           // time.Time
```

TIP

Go to `https://golang.org/pkg/fmt/` for a list of printing verbs supported by Go.

» **Use the `reflect` package.** The `reflect` package allows you to find out the data type of a variable (especially when using interfaces, which I cover in more detail in Chapter 10).

Using the previous example, you can use the `TypeOf()` function to find out the data type of a variable, and the `ValueOf()` and `Kind()` functions to find out the data structure of a variable:

```
fmt.Println(reflect.TypeOf(start))          // time.Time
fmt.Println(reflect.ValueOf(start).Kind()) // struct
```

Converting a variable's type

Very often, you need to convert the value of a variable from one type to another. Consider the following example:

```
var age int
fmt.Print("Please enter your age: ")
fmt.Scanf("%d", &age)
fmt.Println("You entered:", age)
```

In the preceding code snippet, I declared an integer variable age, and then used the Scanf() function to read the input (as an integer as indicated by the %d format specifier) from the console. When you run the program and enter an integer, the program works as expected:

```
$ go run main.go
Please enter your age: 45
You entered: 45
```

However, if you enter a string instead of an integer, this is what you get:

```
$ go run main.go
Please enter your age: forty five
You entered: 0
$ orty five
bash: orty: command not found
```

If you enter a combination of numeric and string values, you see the following:

```
$ go run main.go
Please enter your age: 40-five
You entered: 40
$ five
bash: five: command not found
```

The reason for this behavior is because the Scanf() function scans text read from standard input (the console), storing successive space-separated values into successive arguments as determined by the format specifier. So, in this case, it tries to look for numeric values, and as soon as there is a match, it moves on to the next statement. This is why in the first case, it returns the zero value of age (because there is no numeric value in the input), and in the second case it returns only the first two digits (40). Also, notice that all other unmatched values are brought forward and treated as commands to the command prompt.

To make the program more robust, you may want to change the input variable to a `string` type and read input as a string from the user:

```
var input string
fmt.Print("Please enter your age: ")
fmt.Scanf("%s", &input)
```

The & character represents the memory address of the variable. In this case, it means the Scanf() function reads the user's input and assigns the value to the memory location of the `input` variable.

After the input is read, you can use the `strconv` package's Atoi() function to try to convert the string into an integer value:

```
age, err := strconv.Atoi(input) // convert string to
                                 // int
```

Atoi stands for ASCII to integer. *Itoa*, on the other hand, stands for Integer to ASCII.

The Atoi() function returns two values: the result of the conversion, and the error (if any). To check if an error occurred during the conversion, check if the `err` variable contains a `nil` value:

```
if err != nil {          // an error occurred
    fmt.Println(err)
} else {
    fmt.Println("Your age is:", age)
}
```

To convert string values to specific types, such as Boolean, floating point numbers, or integers, you can use the various `Parse` functions:

```
b, err := strconv.ParseBool("t")
fmt.Println(b)          // true
fmt.Println(err)        // <nil>
fmt.Printf("%T\n", b) // bool

f, err := strconv.ParseFloat("3.1415", 64)
fmt.Println(f)          // 3.1415
fmt.Println(err)        // <nil>
fmt.Printf("%T\n", f) // float64

i, err :=
```

```
    strconv.ParseInt("-18.56", 10, 64) // base
                                        // 10, 64-bit
fmt.Println(i)                          // 0
fmt.Println(err)        // strconv.ParseInt: parsing
                        // "-18.56": invalid syntax
fmt.Printf("%T\n", i)   // int64

u1, err := strconv.ParseUint("18", 10, 64)
fmt.Println(u1)         // 18
fmt.Println(err)        // <nil>
fmt.Printf("%T\n", u1) // uint64

u2, err := strconv.ParseUint("-18", 10, 64)
fmt.Println(u2)         // 0
fmt.Println(err)        // strconv.ParseUint: parsing
                        // "-18": invalid syntax
fmt.Printf("%T\n", u2) // uint64
```

To convert between the various numeric data types like int and float, you can simply use the int(), float32(), and float64() functions:

```
num1 := 5
num2 := float32(num1)
num3 := float64(num2)
num4 := float32(num3)
num5 := int(num4)

fmt.Printf("%T\n", num1) // int
fmt.Printf("%T\n", num2) // float32
fmt.Printf("%T\n", num3) // float64
fmt.Printf("%T\n", num4) // float32
fmt.Printf("%T\n", num5) // int
```

TIP

To find out the range of values representable by each type, go to https://golang. org/ref/spec#Numeric_types.

Interpolating strings

Another common task in programming is printing the values of several variables in a single string. Consider the following:

```
queue := 5
name := "John"
```

Suppose you want to create a string that contains the result like this: `John, your queue number is 5`. But you can't do something like this:

```
s := name + ", your queue number is:" + queue
```

This is because `queue` is an integer, and you can't simply directly concatenate `string` and `integer` values. To fix this, you can convert the `integer` variable value to `string` and then concatenate them:

```
s := name + ", your queue number is:" +
    strconv.Itoa(queue)
```

Although this works, it can turn out to be very unwieldy when you have numerous variables of different types that you need to concatenate.

A better solution is to use the `Sprintf()` function from the `fmt` package:

```
s := fmt.Sprintf("%s, your queue number is %d",
    name, queue)
```

The `Sprintf()` function formats a string based on the formatting verbs (such as `%d` and `%s`).

Chapter **3**

Making Decisions

To make a program really useful, you need to be able to make decisions based on the values of variables and constants. Go offers a few constructs for making decisions:

» If/else statements

» Switch statements

» Select statements

The third construct — the select statement — is for channel communication. I cover that subject in Chapter 12, where I explain more about channels.

In this chapter, I explain how to make decisions in Go using the if/else and switch statements.

Using If/Else Statements to Make Decisions

The first method of making decisions in Go is the if/else statement. An if/else statement basically says, "Do *x* if such-and-such is true; otherwise, do *y*." In the following sections, I walk you through how to use the if/else statement, starting with the foundation of decision making: logical and comparison operators.

Laying the foundation for the if/else statement: Logical and comparison operators

Before I get to the if/else statement, though, you need to know a little bit about how programming works. In Go, a Boolean (bool) variable can take on a value of true or false. This seemingly simple concept is the cornerstone of programming. Boolean values are used in programming to make comparisons and control the flow of programs. Without Boolean variables, there would be no programs!

To get a Boolean value, you usually use a *comparison operator*. Here's a simple example:

```
num := 6
condition := num % 2 == 0
```

In the preceding statements, I'm using the modulo (%) operator to check the remainder of a value divided by 2. If the remainder is 0, num is an even number. The following is a logical expression:

```
num % 2 == 0
```

The result is a Boolean value. It's either true (if num contains an even number) or false (if num contains an odd number).

Table 3-1 shows all the comparison operators supported in Go.

TABLE 3-1

Comparison Operators in Go

Operator	Description	Example
==	Equal to	num == 0
!=	Not equal to	num != 0
<	Less than	num < 0
<=	Less than or equal to	num <= 0
>	Greater than	num > 0
>=	Greater than or equal to	num >= 0

In the following examples, the first line (num := 6) is using the short variable declaration operator (:=), covered in Chapter 2, to basically say, "The variable num is assigned a value of 6." In the following example, I'm using the == operator, which means "equal to." Because 6 is not equal to 0, the result is false.

```
num := 6
fmt.Println(num == 0)   // false
```

In the following example, I'm using the != operator, which means "not equal to." Because 6 is not equal to 0, the result is true.

```
num := 6
fmt.Println(num != 0)   // true
```

In the following example, I'm using the < operator, which means "less than." Because 6 is not less than 0, the result is false.

```
num := 6
fmt.Println(num < 0)    // false
```

In the following example, I'm using the <= operator, which means "less than or equal to." Because 6 is not less than or equal to 0, the result is false.

```
num := 6
fmt.Println(num <= 0)   // false
```

In the following example, I'm using the > operator, which means "greater than." Because 6 is greater than 0, the result is true.

```
num := 6
fmt.Println(num > 0)    // true
```

In the following example, I'm using the >= operator, which means "greater than or equal to." Because 6 is greater than or equal to 0, the result is true.

```
num := 6
fmt.Println(num >= 0)   // true
```

You can *combine* logical expressions using a *logical operator*. Table 3-2 shows all the logical operators supported in Go.

TABLE 3-2   **Logical Operators in Go**

Operator	Description	Example
&&	Logical AND operator. Both operands must be true in order for the condition to evaluate to true.	x && y
||	Logical OR operator. Either operand must be true in order for the condition to evaluate to true.	x || y
!	Logical NOT operator. Reverses the Boolean value — true becomes false and false becomes true.	!x

Here are some examples of logical operators in action. The following code snippet checks if a number is more than 2 *and* less than 9:

```
num := 6
condition := num>2 && num <9
fmt.Println(condition)          // true
```

The following code snippet checks if a number is more than 9 *or* less than 2:

```
num := 6
condition := num>9 || num <2
fmt.Println(condition)          // false
```

The following code snippet checks if a number is between 2 and 9:

```
num := 6
condition := !(num>9 || num <2)
fmt.Println(condition)          //  true
```

Using the if/else statement

You use logical and comparison operators (see the preceding section) to generate a Boolean value so you can make decisions. Like humans, a program makes decisions all the time, and it's precisely this ability that makes computers so powerful. In Go, one way you make decisions is with the if/else statement.

The following code snippet prints the string Number is odd if the condition is true (in other words, if the number is odd):

```
num := 5
condition := num % 2 == 1
if condition {
    fmt.Println("Number is odd")
}
```

You could check the value of the condition explicitly, but this isn't necessary:

```
if condition == true {
    fmt.Println("Number is odd")
}
```

You can also put the logical expression directly in the conditional part of the if statement:

```
if num % 2 == 1 {
    fmt.Println("Number is odd")
}
```

Note that parentheses around conditions are not required, but the braces around the block of statements after the if or else statement are mandatory.

TIP

In the C programming language, a nonzero value is treated as true. So, you may have the following expression in C:

```
if num % 2 {
    ...
}
```

But this doesn't work in Go. If you were to do that in Go, you'd get the following error:

```
non-bool num % 2 (type int) used as if condition
```

When you want to execute code when the condition in an if statement evaluates to false, you use the else statement:

```
if num % 2 == 1 {
    fmt.Println("Number is odd")
} else {
    fmt.Println("Number is even")
}
```

In the preceding code snippet, if the remainder of the number that is divided by 2 is not equal to 1, you print out the sentence Number is even.

Short-circuiting: Evaluating conditions in Go

Go evaluates conditions using a method known as *short-circuiting.* The best way to explain short-circuiting is to use an analogy. Suppose you want to decide whether you have to stay indoors. As long as it's raining *or* it's snowing, you have to stay indoors. To make a decision, you first check whether it's raining. If it *is* raining, you don't have to check if it's snowing anymore because your first condition is already true.

Similarly, suppose you've never experienced this phenomenon of raining *and* snowing at the same time. So, if it rains and snows at the same time, you want to go outdoors and experience this rare event. In this case, if it is currently *not* raining, you don't have to check if it's snowing anymore, because your first condition is already false. So, you don't have to go out.

Here's an example in Go. You have two functions (turn to Chapter 5 for more on functions):

```go
func raining() bool {
    fmt.Println("Check if it is raining now...")
    return true
}

func snowing() bool {
    fmt.Println("Check if it is snowing now...")
    return true
}
```

The following code snippets and outputs demonstrates short-circuiting in action:

```go
if raining() || snowing() {
    fmt.Println("Stay indoors!")
}
/*
Check if it is raining now...
Stay indoors!
*/
```

In this example, because `raining()` returns `true`, you no longer have to call the `snowing()` function.

```
if !raining() || snowing() {
    fmt.Println("Let's ski!")
}
/*
Check if it is raining now...
Check if it is snowing now...
Let's ski!
*/
```

In the preceding example, the first expression (`!raining()`) evaluates to `false`, so you have to evaluate the `snowing()` function:

```
if !raining() && !snowing() {
    fmt.Println("Let's go outdoors!")
}
/*
Check if it is raining now...
*/
```

In the preceding example, because the first expression already evaluates to `false`, there is no need to call the second function (note that I'm using the logical AND operator, &&, here):

```
if raining() && snowing() {
    fmt.Println("It's going to be really cold!")
}
/*
Check if it is raining now...
Check if it is snowing now...
It's going to be really cold!
*/
```

In the preceding example, even though the first condition is `true`, you still need to call the second function in order to ascertain if the entire set of conditions is true.

USING IF WITH AN INITIALIZATION STATEMENT TO KEEP THE SCOPE OF YOUR VARIABLES TIGHT

When using the if statement, you can combine initialization together with the condition statement. Suppose you have a function like this:

```go
func doSomething() (int, bool) {
    //...
    // just an example of some return values
    return 5, false
}
```

The function returns an integer value, together with a Boolean value, to indicate if there is an error code. You usually call this function like this:

```go
v, err := doSomething()
if err {
    // handle the error
} else {
    fmt.Println(v)
}
```

If the function has an error, you handle the error. Otherwise, you can go ahead and use the value returned by the function.

Observe that v and err are used within the if/else statement and are usually not used elsewhere. So, to keep the scope of the variables tight, there is a design pattern that's very popular that Go also supports:

```go
if v, err := doSomething(); !err {
    fmt.Println(v)
} else {
    // handle the error
}
```

In this case, you put the initialization of v and err within the if statement, and then within the same statement you evaluate the value of err:

```go
if v, err := doSomething(); !err {
```

Just remember that the scope of v and err is now limited to within the if/else statement. If you try to access them outside the if/else statement, you'll get an error.

TIP

WHAT ABOUT THE TERNARY OPERATOR?

In some languages (like C and Java), you have the *ternary operator* (?), which takes in three operands. The ternary operator has the following format:

```
res = expr ? x: y
```

So, for example, if you want to check the parity of a number and assign a string to another variable, you can do something like this with the ternary operator:

```
num = 5
// not supported in Go
parity = num % 2 == 0 ? "even" : "odd"
```

However, unfortunately, Go doesn't support the ternary operator. So, you have to resort to doing it the old-fashioned way:

```
num := 5
parity := ""
if num % 2 == 0 {
    parity = "even"
} else {
    parity = "odd"
}
```

A much better solution would be to write a function to do the checks:

```
func checkParity(num int) string {
    if num % 2 == 0 {
        return "even"
    }
    return "odd"
}
...
    num := 5
    parity := checkParity(num)
```

According to the Go Programming Language FAQ (https://golang.org/doc/faq#Does_Go_have_a_ternary_form):

The reason ?: is absent from Go is that the language's designers had seen the operation used too often to create impenetrably complex expressions. The if/else form, although longer, is unquestionably clearer. A language needs only one conditional control flow construct.

When You Have Too Many Conditions: Using the Switch Statement

When you have multiple conditions to evaluate, you'll find yourself writing a lot of if/else statements. And a bunch of if/else statements makes understanding your code much more difficult. A much shorter way is to use a switch statement. A switch statement is passed a variable whose value is compared to each *case* value. When a match is found, the corresponding block of statements is executed.

The following example demonstrates how to use a switch statement:

```
num := 5
dayOfWeek := ""
switch num {
case 1:
dayOfWeek = "Monday"
case 2:
    dayOfWeek = "Tuesday"
case 3:
    dayOfWeek = "Wednesday"
case 4:
    dayOfWeek = "Thursday"
case 5:
    dayOfWeek = "Friday"
case 6:
    dayOfWeek = "Saturday"
case 7:
    dayOfWeek = "Sunday"
default:
    dayOfWeek = "--error--"
}

fmt.Println(dayOfWeek) // Friday
```

In the preceding code snippet, the value of num is first compared to the first case, the value of which is 1. If there is a match, the statement after the colon (:) is executed. If there isn't a match, it continues to the next case until a match is found. If there still isn't a match after the seventh case, the default case will eventually be matched. When a block of statements is executed, control is immediately transferred out of the switch statement.

TIP

If you've programmed in C, keep in mind that there is no need to use a `break` statement at the end of each case.

You can also have multiple statements to execute for each case, as the following code illustrates:

```
switch num {
    case 1:
        dayOfWeek = "Monday"
        fmt.Println("Monday blues...")

    case 2: dayOfWeek = "Tuesday"
    case 3: dayOfWeek = "Wednesday"
    case 4: dayOfWeek = "Thursday"
    case 5:
        dayOfWeek = "Friday"
        fmt.Println("TGIF!!!")

    case 6: dayOfWeek = "Saturday"
    case 7: dayOfWeek = "Sunday"
    default:
}
```

Switching with fall-throughs

When a case is matched in a switch statement, control is transferred out of the switch when the associated block of code is executed. However, there are cases where you *don't* want this default behavior.

Consider the following scenario where you can print a sentence indicating if a student passes his examination. If he scores A, B, C, or D, you print Passed. If he scores F, you print Failed. Otherwise, you print Absent. This scenario can be represented using the switch statement with the `fallthrough` keyword, like this:

```
grade := "C"
switch grade {
    case "A":
        fallthrough
    case "B":
        fallthrough
    case "C":
        fallthrough
    case "D":
```

```
        fmt.Println("Passed")
    case "F":
        fmt.Println("Failed")
    default:
        fmt.Println("Absent")
}
```

When a `fallthrough` keyword is present in the switch statement, the next case is evaluated instead of transferring control out of the switch statement. In the preceding example, `Passed` would be printed.

Matching multiple cases

Instead of using the fallthrough keyword in the example in the previous section, you could also use the case statement to match multiple values, like this:

```
grade := "C"
switch grade {
    case "A", "B", "C", "D":
        fmt.Println("Passed")
    case "F":
        fmt.Println("Failed")
    default:
        fmt.Println("Undefined")
}
```

Switching without condition

You can also write a switch statement without any condition. Consider the following scenario where you have a variable containing the score of an examination. Based on the score, you want to assign a grade based on the following ranges:

>> **Less than 50:** F

>> **50 to 59:** D

>> **60 to 69:** C

>> **70 to 79:** B

>> **80 or higher:** A

Instead of writing a deck of if/else statements, you can do this using the switch statement without the condition:

```
score := 79
grade := ""
switch {
    case score < 50: grade = "F"
    case score < 60: grade = "D"
    case score < 70: grade = "C"
    case score < 80: grade = "B"
    default: grade = "A"
}
fmt.Println(grade)     // B
```

This construct makes it easy to perform conditional checks within the case expressions.

TIP

Unlike in C and Java, the case expressions in Go don't need to be constants.

Chapter **4**

Over and Over and Over: Using Loops

The greatest thing about computers is that, unlike you and me, they can perform tasks repeatedly without getting tired. To support this feature, programming languages use constructs known as *loops* to enable programmers to execute blocks of code repeatedly.

Although programming languages like C and Java have multiple types of looping — while, do...while, and for — Go has only one looping construct: the for loop. But don't let the simplicity fool you: The for loop is powerful enough to meet all your programming needs.

Performing Loops Using the for Statement

In Go, this is what a for statement looks like:

```
for (init; condition; post) {
}
```

This loop has the following three components:

» An init statement: This statement is executed before the first iteration starts. (Each time the for statement executes the statements contained within it is called an *iteration*.)

» A condition expression: This expression is evaluated before the iteration starts to determine if the iteration should continue.

» A post statement: This statement is evaluated at the end of each iteration.

The best way to understand a for loop is with an example:

```
package main

import "fmt"

func main() {
    for i:=0; i<5; i++ {
        fmt.Println(i)
    }
}
```

In the preceding for loop, the init statement consists of the initialization of a variable named i. Before the start of each iteration, the value of i is checked to ensure that it's less than 5 (this is the condition expression). If the condition is true, then the iteration — the block of statement(s) within the for loop — will run. At the end of each iteration, the value of i is incremented by 1 (this is the post statement), and the iteration continues. The iteration stops when the condition statement evaluates to false — that is, when i is no longer less than 5. The preceding code snippet prints out the following output:

```
0
1
2
3
4
```

If you want to print the output in reverse, you can use the following for loop:

```
for i:=4; i>=0; i-- {
    fmt.Println(i)
}
```

And the output will now look like this:

```
4
3
2
1
0
```

A WORD ABOUT ++ AND --

If you're coming from the C and Java camp, you're probably very familiar with the pre- and post-increment/decrement operators:

```
num++   // post-increment operator
++num   // pre-increment operator
num--   // post-decrement operator
--num   // pre-decrement operator
```

Go doesn't have the concept of pre or post operators (which has been a major source of confusion for some programmers). In Go, you can use the ++ or -- operators to increment or decrement a variable's value by 1, respectively.

However, be aware that ++ and -- are *statements,* not *expressions,* so the following statements are valid:

```
x := 5
x++                     // x++ increments value of x by 1;
                        // this is okay
```

And the following statements are *not* valid:

```
++x                     // this is NOT okay; not supported by Go
fmt.Println(x++)        // x++ increments value of x by 1, but
                        // it does not return a result;
                        // hence, this is NOT okay
```

Remember: A *statement* does something, whereas an *expression* is a combination of variables, operations, and values that returns a result.

TIP

Unlike other languages like C, Java, or JavaScript, in Go you don't need to surround the three components of the `for` loop with parentheses. In fact, the following is invalid:

```
for (i:=4; i>= 0; i--) {
    fmt.Println(i)
}
```

TIP

Although a `for` loop technically has three sections (`init`, `condition`, and `post`), the `init` and `post` statements are actually optional. To see an example of this, I've written some code to generate the sequence of Fibonacci numbers up to a certain maximum value:

```
max := 100
a, b := 0, 1
for ;b <= max; {
    println(b)
    a, b = b, a+b
}
```

TECHNICAL STUFF

The Fibonacci sequence is a series of numbers where the next number is the sum of the previous two numbers, starting with 0 and 1. Some sources define the Fibonacci starting with two 1s (https://en.wikipedia.org/wiki/Fibonacci_number). However, apart from the first starting number, the rest of the Fibonacci sequence is the same: 0, 1, 1, 2, 3, 5, 8, 13, 21, 34, . . .

In the previous code snippet, you only have the conditional expression in the `for` loop. You just need to check if `b` is less than or equal to `max` in order for the iteration to continue. When `b` exceeds `max`, the loop stops.

In fact, there is no need for the two semicolons in the `for` loop if the `init` and `post` statements are omitted, so the code could be rewritten like this:

```
for b <= max {
    println(b)
    a, b = b, a+b
}
```

TIP

On careful observation, you may realize that this is actually the `while` loop that so many languages support! In Go, there is no `while` loop, but you can use the `for` loop to improvise it.

INFINITE LOOPS

In programming, an *infinite loop* is a sequence of statements that executes endlessly, unless an external intervention occurs. A for loop without the three parts is an infinite loop:

```
for {
}
```

The following code snippet repeatedly waits for the user to input a string, until the user enters the string QUIT:

```go
package main

import (
    "fmt"
    "strings"
)

func main() {
    for {
        fmt.Println("Enter QUIT to exit")
        var input string
        fmt.Print("Please enter a string:")
        fmt.Scanln(&input)
        if strings.ToUpper(input) == "QUIT" {
            break
        }
    }
}
```

Here's an example of the program in action:

```
$ go run main.go
Enter QUIT to exit
Please enter a string: a
Enter QUIT to exit
Please enter a string: b
Enter QUIT to exit
Please enter a string: quit
$
```

(continued)

(continued)

Notice that you use the ToUpper() function from the strings package to convert the user input to uppercase before you do the comparison. This way, the user can enter the QUIT string in any cases and the comparison will still work correctly.

To exit a for loop, you use the break keyword. The break keyword allows you to terminate the execution of the current loop.

Besides the break keyword, Go also supports the continue keyword. The continue keyword skips the remainder portion of the for loop, returns to the top of the loop, and continues a new iteration. Here's an example where you can make use of the for loop and the continue keyword to print all the odd numbers from 1 to 9:

```go
for n := 1; n < 10; n++ {
    if n%2 == 0 {
        continue
    }
    fmt.Println(n)
}
```

Interestingly, you can reduce the number of lines for the Fibonacci sequence by putting the initialization of a and b into the init part and the assignments of a and b into the post part of the for loop:

```go
max := 100
for a, b := 0, 1; b <= max; a, b = b, a+b {
    println(b)
}
```

Iterating over a Range of Values

Besides using the for statement to perform a set of statements repeatedly, you often use it to iterate through a collection of items, such as arrays/slices or strings. In the following sections, I show you how to use the for statement to iterate through arrays/slices and iterate through strings to extract their characters one by one.

Iterating through arrays/slices

An array/slice is basically a collection of items in Go (you learn more about arrays and slices in Chapter 6).

For example, OS is an array of three elements:

```
var OS [3]string
OS[0] = "iOS"
OS[1] = "Android"
OS[2] = "Windows"
```

To iterate through each of the elements in the array, you use the for-range loop:

```
for i, v := range OS {
    fmt.Println(i, v)
}
```

The range keyword returns the following values:

>> i: The index of the value you're accessing — in this case, the value is the OS array.

>> v: Each of the values in the OS array.

The previous code snippet prints out the following:

```
0 iOS
1 Android
2 Windows
```

If you don't care about the index, you can use a blank identifier:

```
for _, v := range OS {
    fmt.Println(v)
}
```

And, of course, you can do likewise for the value:

```
for i, _ := range OS {
    fmt.Println(i)
}
```

In fact, you can simply omit the blank identifier entirely:

```
for i := range OS {
    fmt.Println(i)
}
```

Iterating through a string

One of the most common operations involving strings is going through each of the characters in a string and finding the characters you want. In Go, a string is essentially a read-only slice of bytes. So, you can use the for-range loop to extract each of the characters in the string. Here's an example:

```
for pos, char := range "Hello, world!" {
    fmt.Println(pos, char)
}
```

The preceding code snippet prints out the following output:

```
0 72
1 101
2 108
3 108
4 111
5 44
6 32
7 119
8 111
9 114
10 108
11 100
12 33
```

You may be a bit surprised by the output. What are all these values like 72, 101, and 108? These values are actually the Unicode code for each character in the string. A Unicode code of 72 is the numerical representation of the *H* character.

TIP

Unicode, which uses numbers to represent characters, is a standard for the encoding, representation, and handling of text. It's a widely used standard for encoding text documents on computers. To see how you get these numbers, go to www. codetable.net.

When you iterate through a string using the for-range loop, the value you get for each character is the Unicode value. If you want to get the actual character itself, use the Printf() function (with the %c format specifier) from the fmt package:

```
for pos, char := range "Hello, world!" {
    fmt.Printf("%d %c\n", pos, char)
}
```

You should now get the following output:

```
0 H
1 e
2 l
3 l
4 o
5 ,
6
7 w
8 o
9 r
10 l
11 d
12 !
```

When your string contains characters that take up more than 1 byte to represent (for example, Chinese and Japanese characters), the index returned by the range keyword actually represents the byte location, as the following example illustrates:

```
for pos, char := range "こんにちは世界" {
    fmt.Printf("%c at byte location %d\n", char, pos)
}
```

The preceding code snippet returns the following output:

```
こ at byte location 0
ん at byte location 3
に at byte location 6
ち at byte location 9
は at byte location 12
世 at byte location 15
界 at byte location 18
```

Using Labels with the for Loop

Earlier, I show how you can use the continue statement to skip an iteration and the break statement to exit a for loop. However, the continue or the break statement only affects the current for loop. What happens if you're in a nested for loop and you want to exit from these two loops altogether? I'll illustrate this with an example.

Consider the following code snippet where you have two nested `for` loops to print out a simple multiplication table from 1 to 5:

```go
for i := 1; i <= 5; i++ {
    for j := 1; j <= 5; j++ {
        fmt.Printf("%d * %d = %d\n", i, j, i*j)
    }
    fmt.Println("------------")
}
```

The preceding code snippet prints out the following output:

```
1 * 1 = 1
1 * 2 = 2
1 * 3 = 3
1 * 4 = 4
1 * 5 = 5
------------
2 * 1 = 2
2 * 2 = 4
2 * 3 = 6
2 * 4 = 8
2 * 5 = 10
------------
3 * 1 = 3
3 * 2 = 6
3 * 3 = 9
3 * 4 = 12
3 * 5 = 15
------------
4 * 1 = 4
4 * 2 = 8
4 * 3 = 12
4 * 4 = 16
4 * 5 = 20
------------
5 * 1 = 5
5 * 2 = 10
5 * 3 = 15
5 * 4 = 20
5 * 5 = 25
------------
```

Suppose you only want to print the multiplication table for 1 and 2, so you insert the block of code in bold:

```
for i := 1; i <= 5; i++ {
    for j := 1; j <= 5; j++ {
        if i == 3 {
            break
        }
        fmt.Printf("%d * %d = %d\n", i, j, i*j)
    }
    fmt.Println("------------")
}
```

However, when you look at the output, you see that it only skips the multiplication table for 3 and continues to print from 4 onward:

```
1 * 1 = 1
1 * 2 = 2
1 * 3 = 3
1 * 4 = 4
1 * 5 = 5
------------
2 * 1 = 2
2 * 2 = 4
2 * 3 = 6
2 * 4 = 8
2 * 5 = 10
------------
------------
4 * 1 = 4
4 * 2 = 8
4 * 3 = 12
4 * 4 = 16
4 * 5 = 20
------------
5 * 1 = 5
5 * 2 = 10
5 * 3 = 15
5 * 4 = 20
5 * 5 = 25
------------
```

What you actually intended was to exit the two for loops totally — both the inner as well as the outer loops. But the break statement only breaks out from the innermost loop that it's in. To fix this, you need to use a label for your outer loop, and then specify where the break statement breaks out to:

```
Outerloop:
    for i := 1; i <= 5; i++ {
        for j := 1; j <= 5; j++ {
            if i == 3 {
                break Outerloop
            }
            fmt.Printf("%d * %d = %d\n", i, j, i*j)
        }
        fmt.Println("------------")
    }
}
```

The modified break statement now breaks out of the outer loop that is specified by the Outerloop label. The output now looks like this:

```
1 * 1 = 1
1 * 2 = 2
1 * 3 = 3
1 * 4 = 4
1 * 5 = 5
------------
2 * 1 = 2
2 * 2 = 4
2 * 3 = 6
2 * 4 = 8
2 * 5 = 10
------------
```

You can also use the label with the continue statement:

```
Outerloop:
    for i := 1; i <= 5; i++ {
        for j := 1; j <= 5; j++ {
            if i == 3 {
                continue Outerloop
            }
            fmt.Printf("%d * %d = %d\n", i, j, i*j)
        }
```

```
        fmt.Println("------------")
    }
}
```

In this example, the continue statement exits from the inner loop and continues on the next iteration on the for loop specified by the Outerloop label. Now the output skips the multiplication table for 3:

```
1 * 1 = 1
1 * 2 = 2
1 * 3 = 3
1 * 4 = 4
1 * 5 = 5
------------
2 * 1 = 2
2 * 2 = 4
2 * 3 = 6
2 * 4 = 8
2 * 5 = 10
------------
4 * 1 = 4
4 * 2 = 8
4 * 3 = 12
4 * 4 = 16
4 * 5 = 20
------------
5 * 1 = 5
5 * 2 = 10
5 * 3 = 15
5 * 4 = 20
5 * 5 = 25
------------
```

Chapter **5**

Grouping Code into Functions

I n programming, you often organize blocks of statements into logical groups called *functions*. Functions allow you to break down a complex task into smaller, more manageable units. They also make it easier for you to reuse your code.

In this chapter, I show you how to write functions in Go, starting from the basics, right up to the more abstract concept known as anonymous functions. I also explain how you can use anonymous functions to implement closures.

Defining a Function

To define a function, you use the `func` keyword, together with the function name, like this:

```
package main

import (
    "fmt"
```

```
        "time"
)

func displayDate() {
    fmt.Println(time.Now().Date())
}
```

In this example, displayDate() is a function that takes in no argument and returns no value. It basically displays the current date. To call the function, simply call its name followed by a pair of parentheses:

```
func main() {
    displayDate()
}
```

When you run the program, it prints out the current date:

```
2020 October 26
```

And now you know what day I wrote this text!

Defining functions with parameters

A function can accept arguments, which you pass to the function when you call it. Here's how you can add a parameter to the displayDate() function (from the previous example):

```
func displayDate(format string) {
    fmt.Println(time.Now().Format(format))
}
```

The parameter, format, is used to format the date and time to be displayed.

TECHNICAL STUFF

You may sometimes see the word *parameter* and *argument* used interchangeably, but they aren't the same thing. A parameter is a variable defined in a function declaration; an argument, on the other hand, is the actual *value* that gets passed to the function.

To call the displayDate() function with an argument, you can pass in a string like the following:

```
displayDate("Mon 2006-01-02 15:04:05")
```

This function call prints the following output (assuming today's date is July 9, 2020, and the time is 6: 51 a.m.):

```
Thu 2020-07-09 06:51:48
```

While I'm on the topic of date/time formatting, I should explain how Go formats dates and times. The format string `Mon 2006-01-02 15:04:05` in Go serves a special function. Go uses a reference date of Monday, January 2, 2006, at 15:04:05 MST, to represent the various components of a given date and time. Table 5-1 shows the use of each component of the format string and some examples of how to use them.

TABLE 5-1 The Reference Date Used by Go for Formatting Dates and Times

Reference Value	Description	Example Usage
Mon	Day of the week	Mon, Monday
Jan	Month	Jan, January, 01
2	Day	2, 02
15	Hour	15, 3
04	Minute	04, 4
05	Second	05, 5
2006	Year	2006
MST	Time zone	MST

Table 5-2 shows how the current date and time will look using the different format strings and using the date of July 9, 2020, at 06:51:48 (GMT+8) as an example.

TABLE 5-2 The Output of a Date Based on the Date Formatting

Example	Output	Description
displayDate("2006-01-02 15:04:05")	2020-07-09 06:51:48	The date and time are displayed.
displayDate("15:04:05, 2006-Jan-02 Mon")	06:51:48, 2020-Jul-09 Thu	The day of the week (Thu) and month (Jul) are displayed.

(continued)

TABLE 5-2 *(continued)*

Example	Output	Description
`displayDate("15:04:05, 2006-Jan-02 Monday")`	06:51:48, 2020-Jul-09 Thursday	The day of the week is displayed in full.
`displayDate("15:04:05, 2006-January-02 MST Mon")`	06:51:48, 2020-July-09 +08 Thu	The month is displayed in full; the time zone is also displayed (+08).
`displayDate("3:4:05, 2006-1-02 MST Mon")`	6:51:48, 2020-7-09 +08 Thu	The time zone (+8) is displayed; a single digit is used for the hour.
`displayDate("3:4:05 pm, 2006-1-02 MST Mon")`	6:51:48 am, 2020-7-09 +08 Thu	Morning is displayed as am.
`displayDate("3:4:05 PM, 2006-1-02 MST Mon")`	6:51:48 AM, 2020-7-09 +08 Thu	Morning is displayed as AM.

Defining functions with multiple parameters

A function can have multiple parameters. Using the previous example, you can add one more parameter to the `displayDate()` function:

```go
func displayDate(format string, prefix string) {
    fmt.Println(prefix, time.Now().Format(format))
}
```

And when you now call the function, just pass it another argument:

```go
displayDate("Mon 2006-01-02 15:04:05",
            "Current Date and Time:")
```

REMEMBER Unlike other languages, like Java and C#, Go does not support *function overloading* (a feature of a programming language that allows you to have multiple functions with the same name but with different signatures [parameters]). Because the design philosophy behind Go is to keep the language simple, it doesn't support function overloading.

Passing arguments by value and by pointer

Consider the following function, `swap()`, where it has two parameters, both of type `int`:

```
func swap(a, b int) {
    a, b = b, a
}
```

Within the function, you swap the values of these two parameters. Now I'll call this function with two variables, x and y:

```
func main() {
    x := 5
    y := 6
    swap(x, y)
    fmt.Println(x, y) // 5 6
}
```

Notice that when the function returns, both the values of x and y are still the same. Aren't they supposed to swap? Why haven't they? When you call the swap() function, the values of x and y are copied into the variables a and b (see Figure 5-1).

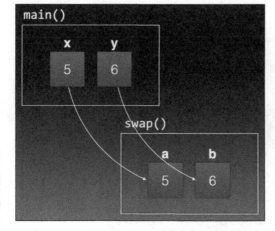

So, whatever happened in the swap() function won't affect the value of x and y in the main() function. This situation is called *passing by value.*

But what if you want the changes made in the swap() function to affect the variables in the main() function? You can modify the parameters in the swap() function to take in pointers to int instead, like this:

```
func swap(a, b *int) {
    *a, *b = *b, *a
}
```

In this modification, a and b now take in the address of memory locations containing int values (as represented by *int). This is known as *passing by pointer* (in some languages this is called *passing by reference*). The following statement means, "Go to the memory location pointed by b and assign its value to the memory location pointed by a":

```
*a, *b = *b, *a
```

Likewise, you also go to the memory location pointed by a and assign the value to the memory location pointed by b.

When you now call the swap() function from main(), you have to pass in the address of x and y using the & operator, which represents "the address of":

```
x := 5
y := 6
swap(&x, &y)
```

Figure 5-2 shows that now a and b are essentially pointing to the original x and y variables.

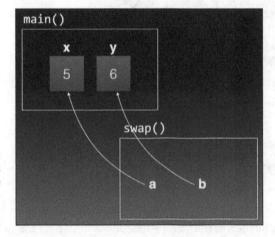

FIGURE 5-2: The addresses of x and y are passed to a and b when the swap() function is called.

Any changes made in the swap() function will now be reflected in x and y when the function exits:

```
x := 5
y := 6
swap(&x, &y)
fmt.Println(x, y) // 6 5
```

Returning values from functions

A function can return values. Consider the following function, addNum( ), which has two parameters and returns a value of type int:

```go
func addNum(num1, num2 int) int {  // returns int
    return num1 + num2
}
```

When you call this function, the returning result can be assigned to another variable:

```go
s := addNum(5, 6)
fmt.Println(s) // 11
```

In Go, a function can return multiple results. To indicate that the function returns multiple values, wrap the types of all returning results with a pair of parentheses, like this:

```go
func countOddEven(s string) (int,int) {
    odds, evens := 0,0
    for _, c := range s {
        if int(c) % 2 == 0 {
            evens++
        } else {
            odds++
        }
    }
    return odds,evens
}
```

When you call a function that returns multiple values, you have to use the exact number of variables to store the returning results:

```go
o, e := countOddEven("12345")
fmt.Println(o,e) // 3 2
```

If there are parts of the result that you want to ignore, use the blank identifier (_):

```go
_, e := countOddEven("12345")
fmt.Println(e) // 2
```

Naming return values

Instead of specifying the type(s) of returning result(s), Go also allows you to name the returning values:

```go
func addNum(num1 int, num2 int) (sum int) {
    sum = num1 + num2
    return  // you can still use "return sum"
}
```

In this example, the returning variable is named sum. This variable is used within the function and at the end of the function. The return statement without any argument will return the value of this variable.

TIP

Using named return values makes your function declaration much more descriptive.

Working with variadic functions

A variadic function takes in a variable number of arguments. The most common variadic function is the fmt.Println() function:

```go
fmt.Println("Hello")
fmt.Println("Hello", "World!")
fmt.Println("Hello", 123, true)
```

To define a function that accepts a variable number of arguments, you use ellipses (...), like this:

```go
func addNums(nums ... int) int {
    total := 0
    for _, n := range nums {
        total += n
    }
    return total
}
```

Essentially, nums is now a slice of int values. You can now call the addNums() function with a variable number of arguments:

```go
fmt.Println(addNums(1,2,3,4,5)) // 15
fmt.Println(addNums(1,2,3))     // 6
```

You can also have a fixed parameter together with a variadic parameter:

```go
func addNums(total int, nums ...int) int {
    fmt.Printf("%T", nums)
    for _, n := range nums {
        total += n
    }
    return total
}
```

However, the variadic parameter must always be the *last* parameter in the function. The following function declaration is not valid:

```go
func addNums(nums ...int, total int) int {
    ...
}
```

Using Anonymous Functions

Go supports a special type of function known as an *anonymous function*. As the name implies, an anonymous function is a function without a name. I'll explain this with an example and show you how anonymous functions can be useful.

Declaring an anonymous function

Earlier, I show you how to declare variables with specific types. I also show you how to declare variables to be of a function type. Consider the following example:

```go
package main

import "fmt"

func main() {
    var i func() int
}
```

Here, you declare i to be a function that returns an int value. For i to be really useful, you need to assign it a function. You can assign it a regular function, like this:

```go
func doSomething() int {
    return 5
}

func main() {
    var i func() int
    i = doSomething
}
```

Or you can assign it an anonymous function, like this:

```go
var i func() int
i = func() int {
    return 5
}
```

In the preceding example, i is assigned an anonymous function. To invoke the anonymous function, call i the way you call a regular function:

```go
func main() {
    var i func() int
    i = func() int {
        return 5
    }
    fmt.Println(i())    // 5
}
```

Implementing closure using anonymous functions

An anonymous function can form a *closure* (a function value that references variables from outside its body). As usual, an example is worth much more than a page of explanation. Consider the following example:

```go
func fib() func() int {
    f1 := 0
    f2 := 1
    return func() int {
        f1, f2 = f2, (f1 + f2)
```

```
        return f1
    }
}
```

The `fib()` function returns a function that returns an `int`. In this case, the `fib()` function returns a closure (which is actually an anonymous function; see Figure 5-3).

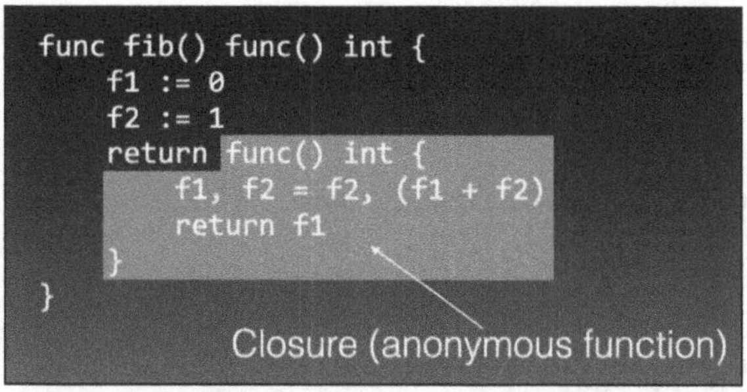

FIGURE 5-3: Implementing a closure using an anonymous function.

```
func fib() func() int {
    f1 := 0
    f2 := 1
    return func() int {
        f1, f2 = f2, (f1 + f2)
        return f1
    }
}
```
Closure (anonymous function)

What makes this anonymous function a closure is that it can access the variables f1 and f2 that are declared outside the function.

You can now assign the `fib()` function to a variable:

```
func main() {
    gen := fib()
}
```

Essentially, gen is referencing the function:

```
func() int {
    f1, f2 = f2, (f1 + f2)
    return f1
}
```

If you now call gen as a function, it returns the first number in the Fibonacci sequence:

```
func main() {
    gen := fib()
    fmt.Println(gen())  // 1
}
```

If you call the gen() function one more time, it returns the second number in the Fibonacci sequence:

```
func main() {
    gen := fib()
    fmt.Println(gen())   // 1
    fmt.Println(gen())   // 1
}
```

The interesting thing about closure is that statements inside the closure can access variables that are outside it. In this example, f1 and f2 are used to hold the last two numbers in the Fibonacci sequence.

If you want to access the first ten numbers in the Fibonacci sequence, you can use a for loop:

```
func main() {
    gen := fib()
    for i := 0; i < 10; i++ {
        fmt.Println(gen())
    }
}
```

If you think about it, the beauty of the fib() function is that it generates Fibonacci numbers on demand — it doesn't have to store all the numbers generated. It only stores the last two numbers of the Fibonacci numbers at any given time.

Implementing the filter() function using closure

Most programming languages that support closures come with predefined filter(), map(), and reduce() functions. These functions are paradigms of functional programming. They allow developers to write simpler and shorter code without needing to get into the details of how it's done. Here's what each of these three functions do:

>> The filter() function takes in a collection of items and returns another collection containing the items you want.

>> The map() function allows you to "map" items from one collection into another collection.

>> The reduce() function returns a single value based on the collection you pass in.

Unfortunately, Go doesn't come with these predefined functions. But here's how to implement the `filter()` function using closure:

```
func filter(arr []int, cond func(int) bool) []int {
    result := []int{}
    for _, v := range arr {
        if cond(v) {
            result = append(result, v)
        }
    }
    return result
}
```

The `filter()` function takes in two arguments:

>> A slice of `int`

>> A function with a single `int` parameter and return value of type `bool`

The function returns a slice of `int`. Within the function, you iterate through each of the numbers in the slice of `int`, and if the result of the anonymous function (cond) evaluates to `true`, you append the number to another slice (`result`).

To use this `filter()` function, you can pass it an array as the first argument and pass an anonymous function as the second argument (bolded for emphasis):

```
func main() {
    a := []int{1, 2, 3, 4, 5}
    evens := filter(a,
        func(val int) bool {
            return val%2 == 0
        })
    fmt.Println(evens)
}
```

The preceding code snippet prints out all the even numbers from the array a:

```
[2 4]
```

What about printing all the numbers greater than 3? Easy, just change the condition in the anonymous function:

```go
func main() {
    a := []int{1, 2, 3, 4, 5}
    evens := filter(a,
        func(val int) bool {
            return val > 3
        })
    fmt.Println(evens)
}
```

The output will now contain all numbers greater than 3:

```
[4 5]
```

2

Working with Data Structures

IN THIS PART . . .

Create collections of items using arrays and slices.

Group related variables together with structs.

Use maps to create associative arrays of items.

Understand the JSON data format and how to encode and decode it to Go structs.

Create method signatures using interfaces.

Chapter **6**

Slicing and Dicing Using Arrays and Slices

n Chapter 2, I show you how to declare variables and constants to use the various basic data types in Go — int, bool, float32, and so on. In real-life applications, you usually need to deal with *collections* of data. For example, you may need to store the temperature of a city for the past 30 days, so you need to store a collection of 30 floating-point numbers. This is where array comes in.

In this chapter, I explain how to use arrays to store collections of items. I also introduce you to another related data structure: slices. Together, arrays and slices provide a very flexible way to manipulate collections of data.

Arming Yourself to Use Arrays

In Go, an *array* is a numbered sequence of items of a specific length. Think of arrays as collections of items of the same type, such as the ones shown in Figure 6-1.

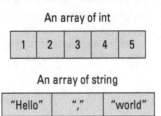

An array of int

| 1 | 2 | 3 | 4 | 5 |

An array of string

| "Hello" | "," | "world" |

FIGURE 6-1:
An array is a
collection of
items of the
same type.

The values an array holds are known as its *items* or *elements*. In Go, all the elements in an array must be of the same type. After an array is created, the array can't change in size — it can't grow or shrink.

In the following sections, I show you how to declare and initialize arrays in Go. I also introduce you to multidimensional arrays.

Declaring an array

To declare an array, you use the following syntax:

```
var array_name [size_of_array]data_type
```

The following program declares an array called `nums` of type `int` with five elements:

```go
package main

import (
    "fmt"
)

func main() {
    var nums [5]int    // an array of int (5 elements)
    fmt.Println(nums) // [0 0 0 0 0]

}
```

When you print out `nums`, you see its zero values:

```
[0 0 0 0 0]
```

REMEMBER

The `nums` array will hold *exactly* five elements. The index (the position of the elements in the array) of elements in arrays in Go are zero-based, which means to access the first element in an array, you use 0 as the index:

```
fmt.Println(nums[0])    // first element
fmt.Println(nums[1])    // second element
```

Initializing an array

When declaring an array, you can also initialize it to some initial values. To do so, you just supply the initial values with an *array literal*, as in the following example:

```
nums := [5]int{1, 2, 3, 4, 5}
fmt.Println(nums)
```

The preceding example declares an array named nums and initializes it with the elements {1,2,3,4,5}. Figure 6-2 shows the array created, with the index for each element in the array.

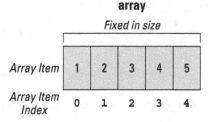

FIGURE 6-2:
An array with five integer elements and its index.

When initializing an array with an array literal, you can omit the length of the size by using the . . . notation:

```
nums := [...]int{1, 2, 3, 4, 5}
```

To get the length of an array, use the len() function (*len* is short for *length*):

```
fmt.Println(len(nums)) // 5
```

Working with multidimensional arrays

The arrays that I show you in the previous sections are one-dimensional. But arrays can also be multidimensional — two-dimensional, three-dimensional, and so on. The best way to visualize a two-dimensional array is to imagine it as a table (see Figure 6-3).

2D array

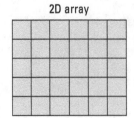

FIGURE 6-3:
Imagining a
two-dimensional
array in Go.

In Figure 6-3, you have a two-dimensional array of five rows and six columns, for a total of 30 elements. The following code snippet shows how to create this two-dimensional array of type `string`, and then populate each element in the array with the row and column numbers:

```
var table [5][6]string
for row := 0; row < 5; row++ {
    for column := 0; column < 6; column++ {
        table[row][column] =
            strconv.Itoa(row) + "," +
                strconv.Itoa(column)
    }
}
fmt.Println(table)
```

When you print out the two-dimensional array, you see the following output (for-matted for clarity):

```
[[0,0 0,1 0,2 0,3 0,4 0,5]
 [1,0 1,1 1,2 1,3 1,4 1,5]
 [2,0 2,1 2,2 2,3 2,4 2,5]
 [3,0 3,1 3,2 3,3 3,4 3,5]
 [4,0 4,1 4,2 4,3 4,4 4,5]]
```

If you want to visualize a three-dimensional array, you can imagine it to be a rectangular prism, as shown in Figure 6-4.

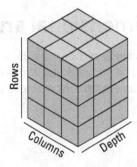

Rows
Columns
Depth

FIGURE 6-4:
Imagining
a three-
dimensional
array in Go.

The following code snippet shows how to create a three-dimensional array in Go:

```go
var cube [4][3][3]string
for row := 0; row < 4; row++ {
    for column := 0; column < 3; column++ {
        for depth := 0; depth < 3; depth++ {
            cube[row][column][depth] =
                strconv.Itoa(row) +
                    strconv.Itoa(column) +
                    strconv.Itoa(depth)
        }
    }
}
fmt.Println(cube)
```

The output of the preceding code snippet looks like this (formatted for clarity):

```
[
    [
        [000 001 002]
        [010 011 012]
        [020 021 022]
    ]
    [
        [100 101 102]
        [110 111 112]
        [120 121 122]
    ]
    [
        [200 201 202]
        [210 211 212]
        [220 221 222]
    ]
    [
        [300 301 302]
        [310 311 312]
        [320 321 322]
    ]
]
```

Figure 6-5 shows how the output correlates with the cube.

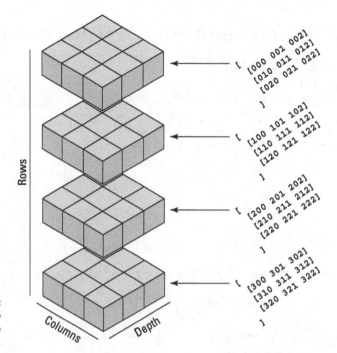

{
  [000 001 002]
  [010 011 012]
  [020 021 022]
}

{
  [100 101 102]
  [110 111 112]
  [120 121 122]
}

{
  [200 201 202]
  [210 211 212]
  [220 221 222]
}

{
  [300 301 302]
  [310 311 312]
  [320 321 322]
}

Rows

Columns   Depth

FIGURE 6-5:
Visualizing the
output of the
code snippet.

Sleuthing Out the Secrets of Slices

Although you can use arrays to store collections of items, another related key data structure that is more commonly used to store collections of items is a *slice*. A slice is just like an array, but unlike an array, it has the ability to grow or shrink in size. Simple enough?

In the following sections, I show you how to create an empty slice, create a slice with initial values, and append items to a slice.

Creating an empty slice

To create a slice, you can use the make() function. The following statement creates a slice of five integer values:

```
s := make([]int, 5)
```

When you print it out:

```
fmt.Println(s)
```

The output is just like that of an array:

```
[0 0 0 0 0]
```

However, this is where the similarity with arrays ends. Whereas an array is fixed in size, a slice is more flexible — the size of a slice can change as you append items to or remove items from it.

Technically, a slice is a view into an underlying array (see Figure 6-6). A slice is represented by a *slice header*, which contains three fields:

>> `ptr`: A pointer that points to the address of the underlying array

>> `len`: The length of the slice

>> `cap`: The *capacity*, or maximum number of allowed elements in the array

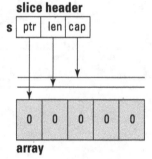

FIGURE 6-6:
A slice is represented by a slice header, which contains three fields.

To find out the length and capacity of the slice s, you use the `len()` and `cap()` functions, respectively:

```
fmt.Println(len(s)) // 5
fmt.Println(cap(s)) // 5
```

In the case of s, you can see that the capacity of s is five items, and at the moment it has five values. If you want to create a slice with a specific length and capacity, you can specify that in the `make()` function, like this:

```
r := make([]int, 2, 5)
fmt.Println(len(r)) // 2
fmt.Println(cap(r)) // 5
```

The preceding code snippet creates a slice, r, with two elements and a capacity of five elements (see Figure 6-7).

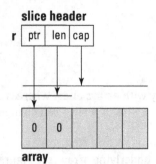

FIGURE 6-7:
A slice with
two elements
and a capacity of
five elements.

Creating and initializing a slice

As with arrays, you can create and initialize a slice with an *array literal* (a list of zero or more elements):

```
t := []int{1, 2, 3, 4, 5}
fmt.Println(len(t)) // 5
fmt.Println(cap(t)) // 5
```

The preceding code snippet creates a slice, t, with the elements, length, and capacity as shown in Figure 6-8.

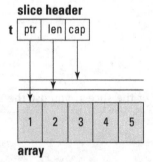

FIGURE 6-8:
A slice created
with initial values.

Appending to a slice

To append an item to a slice, you use the append() function:

```
t = append(t, 6, 7, 8)
```

When you now print out the values of t, you get the following:

```
fmt.Println(t)
// [1 2 3 4 5 6 7 8]
```

This result is expected because you've just added three more elements to the t slice. If you now print out the length and capacity of the slice t, the output may surprise you a little:

```
fmt.Println(len(t)) // 8
fmt.Println(cap(t)) // 10
```

Turns out that when a slice has reached its capacity, appending more items to it causes the slice to point to a *new* underlying array. All the existing items in the slice are copied onto the new array, together with the newly added items. At the same time, the newly created underlying array will now have a bigger capacity (see Figure 6-9).

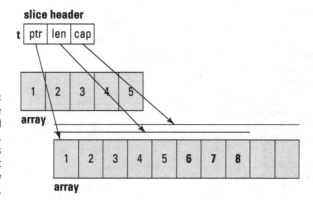

FIGURE 6-9: When a slice has reached its capacity, appending items to it will cause it to point to a new underlying array.

TIP

For efficiency reasons, different versions of Go have different implementations of how the new capacity of the underlying array is determined. However, most of the time, this shouldn't affect your usage of slices.

You can now append two more items to t without causing the underlying array to change (see Figure 6-10):

```
t = append(t, 9, 10)
fmt.Println(len(t)) // 10
fmt.Println(cap(t)) // 10
```

Let's now assign the slice t to another variable named u:

```
u := t
fmt.Println(u) // [1 2 3 4 5 6 7 8 9 10]
fmt.Println(t) // [1 2 3 4 5 6 7 8 9 10]
```

FIGURE 6-10:
You can add
two more items
to t without
exceeding its
capacity.

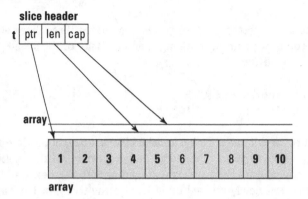

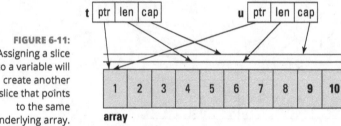

FIGURE 6-10:
You can add
two more items
to t without
exceeding its
capacity.

At this moment, both u and t are pointing to the same underlying array (see Figure 6-11).

FIGURE 6-11:
Assigning a slice
to a variable will
create another
slice that points
to the same
underlying array.

To prove this, let's modify the last element of u and then print out the values of both t and u:

```
u[9] = 100
fmt.Println(u) // [1 2 3 4 5 6 7 8 9 100]
fmt.Println(t) // [1 2 3 4 5 6 7 8 9 100]
```

As the output shows, both u and t have the same elements after the modification (see Figure 6-12), proving that u and t are both pointing to the same underlying array.

Now, let's add a new item to the slice t and print out the values of both u and t:

```
t = append(t, 11)
fmt.Println(u) // [1 2 3 4 5 6 7 8 9 100]
fmt.Println(t) // [1 2 3 4 5 6 7 8 9 100 11]
```

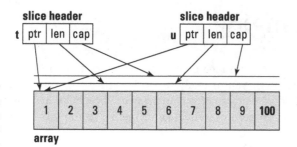

FIGURE 6-12:
Modifying the slice u will also affect slice t.

array

Notice that only t has the newly added item while u remains unchanged. This is because when you added the new item to t, it exceeded its capacity, so a new underlying array was created to accommodate it (see Figure 6-13).

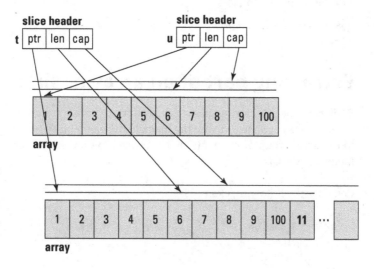

FIGURE 6-13:
Appending an item to t will cause it to exceed its capacity and point to a new array.

array

array

More important, t and u are now pointing to two different underlying arrays. You can verify this by printing the length and capacity of u and t:

```
fmt.Println(len(u)) // 10
fmt.Println(cap(u)) // 10

fmt.Println(len(t)) // 11
fmt.Println(cap(t)) // 20
```

Slicing and Ranging

When you have a solid idea of how arrays and slices are implemented (see the previous sections), you're ready to work with them. You already know how to extract individual elements from an array or slice, but you often need to extract a *range* of values instead of individual elements. In the following sections, I show you how to

>> Use slicing to extract a range of elements.

>> Iterate through arrays and slices.

>> Make copies of arrays and slices.

>> Insert items into slices.

>> Delete items from slices.

Extracting part of an array or slice

Earlier, in the "Declaring an array" section, I show you how to extract elements from an array or slice by using the index of the element. In real life, you often need to extract a group of elements, not just one. To do that, you can use a technique known as *slicing*.

Consider the following example:

```
var c [3]string
c[0] = "iOS"
c[1] = "Android"
c[2] = "Windows"
```

This code snippet has an array named c with three elements. To extract the first two elements, you can use slicing by specifying a *half-open range*, like this:

```
fmt.Println(c[0:2]) // [iOS Android]
```

TIP

A half-open range is one that includes the first element, but excludes the last one. Mathematically, a half-open range is usually written as [*n,m*). For example, [1,5) consists of the values 1, 2, 3, and 4. In Go, half-open values are represented as *n* : *m*.

The first number indicates the starting index of the element to extract, while the number after the colon (:) indicates the end index (not inclusive). So, 0:2 means extract all the items from index 0 through 1. If the starting index is 0, you can simply leave it out, like this:

```
fmt.Println(c[:2])  // [iOS Android]
```

If you want to extract from a particular index through the end, you can leave out the second number in the half-open range:

```
fmt.Println(c[1:])  // [Android Windows]
```

If you want all the elements in the array, you just need to specify the colon:

```
fmt.Println(c[:])   // [iOS Android Windows]
```

REMEMBER

The result of slicing an array is a slice — that is, the result is a new slice pointing to the original array. The same theory applies to slicing a slice — the end result is still a slice.

One thing you need to take note of when slicing is the length and capacity of the resultant slice. Consider another example:

```
t := []int{1, 2, 3, 4, 5}
fmt.Println(len(t))    // 5
fmt.Println(cap(t))    // 5
```

If you try to perform slicing on the slice t and then assign the result back to t:

```
t = t[2:4]
```

You should note that t will now be updated to point to the third element of the underlying array and its length and capacity updated (see Figure 6-14). This can be verified with the following statements:

```
fmt.Println(t)         // [3 4]
fmt.Println(len(t))    // 2
fmt.Println(cap(t))    // 3
```

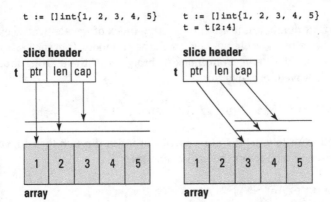

FIGURE 6-14:
Slicing a slice and assigning back the result to the original slice.

In particular, the capacity of the resultant slice will depend on the start index of the first element of the slice. If you slice from 1:3, then your capacity will change (see Figure 6-15).

```
t = t[1:3]
fmt.Println(t)        // [2 3]
fmt.Println(len(t))   // 2
fmt.Println(cap(t))   // 4
```

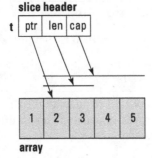

FIGURE 6-15:
The capacity of the slice changes after performing the slicing.

REMEMBER

Whether you're slicing an array or a slice, the result is always a slice.

Iterating through a slice

To iterate through an array or slice, you can use the `for-range` loop (see Chapter 4):

```
for i, v := range t {
    fmt.Println(i, v)
}
```

When you range over an array or slice, two values are returned: the index of the element, and its corresponding value. The preceding code snippet prints out the following output:

```
0 1
1 2
2 3
3 4
4 5
```

Making copies of an array or slice

Occasionally, you need to create copies of your arrays or slices so that you can work on one copy and not affect the original copy.

For arrays, making a copy is very straightforward: Simply assign it to another variable, and a copy is created for you. Consider the following example:

```
nums1 := [5]int{1, 2, 3, 4, 5}
```

If you assign `nums1` to another variable, say `nums2`, `nums2` is now a copy of `nums1`:

```
nums2 := nums1
```

To verify this, print out the values of both `nums1` and `nums2`, and you should see the same output:

```
fmt.Println(nums1) // 1 2 3 4 5]
fmt.Println(nums2) // 1 2 3 4 5]
```

If you now make some changes to nums2, the changes should only affect nums2 and not nums1. The following output proves this point:

```
nums2[0] = 0
fmt.Println(nums1) // 1 2 3 4 5]
fmt.Println(nums2) // 0 2 3 4 5]
```

Although you can simply assign an array to another variable to make a copy of the array, the same technique does not work on slices.

Assigning a slice to a new variable will create another slice that points to the same array pointed to by the original slice. To create copy of slices, use the copy() function. The copy() function has the following syntax:

```
copy(destination, source)
```

To see how this works, suppose you have the following slice t:

```
t := []int{1, 2, 3, 4, 5}
```

Before you can make a copy of this slice, you need to create a slice of the same size:

```
v := make([]int, len(t))
```

You can now use the copy() function to copy the content of the slice t into the slice v:

```
copy(v, t)
fmt.Println(t)  // [1 2 3 4 5]
fmt.Println(v)  // [1 2 3 4 5]
```

Note that the copy() function examines the length of both the destination and source slices and copies the minimum of these two numbers of elements. For example, if v has a length of two and capacity of five, like this:

```
t := []int{1, 2, 3, 4, 5}
v := make([]int, 2, 5)
```

Copying t into v will get you the following:

```
copy(v, t)
fmt.Println(t) // [1 2 3 4 5]
fmt.Println(v) // [1 2]
```

On the other hand, if v now has a length of 10, like this:

```
v := make([]int, 10)
```

Then copying t into v will get you the following:

```
copy(v, t)
fmt.Println(t) // [1 2 3 4 5]
fmt.Println(v) // [1 2 3 4 5 0 0 0 0 0]
```

Inserting an item into a slice

Go doesn't have built-in functions for inserting items into a slice. To do this, you need to implement it yourself using the append() function. Let's define a function called insert(), with the following signature:

```
func insert(orig []int, index int, value int)
    ([]int, error) {
}
```

This function takes in three parameters: the slice to insert the item, the index in the slice to insert the new item, and the value of the item to be inserted. This function returns the modified slice, as well as an error (if there is one). There are three scenarios for inserting an element:

» The index specified is less than 0. In this case, return an error.

» The index is greater than the length of the original slice. In this case, append the item to the end of the slice and return the modified slice.

» The index is within the range of the slice. In this case, insert the item in the slice and return the modified slice.

Suppose you want to insert a new value into index, which is 2 in the example (see Figure 6-16). Follow these steps:

1. Slice all the items from [:index+1], and all the items from [index:].

2. Append the items that you've sliced from [index:] to the items from [:index+1].

3. Replace the value at index with the value that you want to insert (which is 9 in the example).

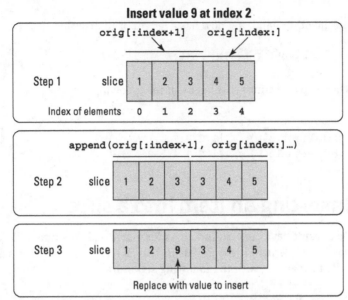

FIGURE 6-16:
Inserting an item
into a slice.

You can now fill in the code for the insert() function:

```
func insert(orig []int, index int, value int)
    ([]int, error) {
    if index < 0 {
        return nil, errors.New(
            "Index cannot be less than 0")
    }

    if index >= len(orig) {
        return append(orig, value), nil
    }

    orig = append(orig[:index+1], orig[index:]...)
    orig[index] = value
    return orig, nil
}
```

Notice the . . . at the end of the append() function. The append() function is a *variadic function* — the second parameter takes in a variable number of arguments. So, when calling the append() function, because you're passing in a slice in the second argument, you need to unpack it with the . . . notation before passing it to the append() function.

You can now test the function, like this:

```
t := []int{1, 2, 3, 4, 5}
t, err := insert(t, 2, 9)
if err == nil {
    fmt.Println(t)    // 1 2 9 3 4 5]
} else {
    fmt.Println(err)
}
```

Removing an item from a slice

Removing an item from a slice is similar to adding an item to a slice, except it's more straightforward. Suppose you want to delete the item at index, which is 2 in the example (see Figure 6-17). Follow these steps:

1. **Slice all the items from** [:index] **and all the items from** [index+1:].

2. **Append the items that you've sliced from** [index+1:] **to the items from** [:index].

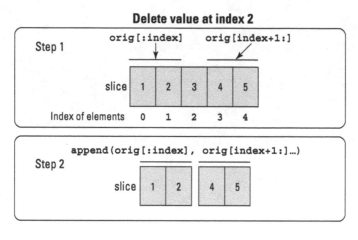

FIGURE 6-17: Removing an item from a slice.

Here is the delete() function to delete an item from a slice:

```
func delete(orig []int, index int) ([]int, error) {
    if index < 0 || index >= len(orig) {
        return nil, errors.New("Index out of range")
    }
```

```
        orig = append(orig[:index], orig[index+1:]...)
        return orig, nil
}
```

You can now test the delete() function:

```
t := []int{1, 2, 3, 4, 5}
t, err := delete(t, 2)
if err == nil {
    fmt.Println(t)      // [1 2 4 5]
} else {
    fmt.Println(err)
}
```

Chapter **7**

Defining the Blueprints of Your Data Using Structs

I n the previous chapter, I tell you all about arrays and slices and show you how to group a collection of items together as a single unit. In this chapter, I fill you in on another way to represent your data: a struct. A *struct* (short for *structure*) is a used-defined type that allows you to group related data into a single logical unit. Here, I show you how to define and initialize a struct, make copies of a struct, define methods in a struct, and compare structs.

Defining Structs for a Collection of Items

Consider the following scenarios where you want to store the location of a point in a two-dimensional (2D) coordinate space. The x- and y-coordinates of the point can simply be stored using two variables:

```
pt1X := 3.1
pt1Y := 5.7
```

If you have another point, you have another set of variables:

```
pt2X := 5.6
pt2Y := 3.8
```

You're using two variables to store the coordinates of a point: *x* and *y*. Because these two coordinates are related, being able to store them as a single variable, rather than two variables, helps.

But what about when you want to store a point in the three-dimensional (3D) coordinate space, like this:

```
pt1X := 3.1
pt1Y := 5.7
pt1Z := 4.2
```

Here, you use another variable to store the *z*-coordinate. A more logical approach would be to group these coordinates into a single variable, and this is where structs in Go comes in handy.

The following program defines a struct named `point` with three *fields* (variables in a struct):

```
package main

import "fmt"

type point struct {
    x float32
    y float32
    z float32
}

func main() {
}
```

The fields in a struct don't need to be of the same type.

To create a variable of `point` type, you can use the `var` keyword just as you would create an `int` or `string` variable, like this:

```
var pt1 point
```

Each field in the struct can then be initialized individually:

```go
func main() {
    var pt1 point
    pt1.x = 3.1
    pt1.y = 5.7
    pt1.z = 4.2
}
```

You can also access the value of each field individually:

```go
fmt.Println(pt1.x)
fmt.Println(pt1.y)
fmt.Println(pt1.z)
```

Another way to create and initialize a struct is using a *struct literal* (created by specifying the values of its fields):

```go
pt2 := point{x: 5.6, y: 3.8, z: 6.9}
```

The field names can be omitted. Values will be assigned to the fields in the order specified. All field values must be specified, though:

```go
pt2 := point{5.6, 3.8, 6.9}
```

TIP

If you want to split the struct literal over multiple lines, make sure there is a comma after the last field:

```go
pt2 := point{
    x: 5.6,
    y: 3.8,
    z: 6.9,     // <-- comma here
}
```

You can also leave out a specific field when initializing the struct:

```go
pt3 := point{x: 5.6, y: 3.8}
```

Fields that are omitted during initialization will be zero-based:

```go
fmt.Println(pt2)    // {5.6 3.8 6.9}
fmt.Println(pt3)    // {5.6 3.8 0}
```

Creating a Go Struct

In the preceding section, I explain the basics of structs — how to create one and initialize the various fields in the structs. For a struct, using *constructor functions* to create a new struct is idiomatic.

TECHNICAL STUFF

Unlike other languages like C# and Java, Go has no default *constructors* (specialized functions used to initialize objects). In Go, creating functions to create and initialize structs is *idiomatic* (meaning it follows the style of writing Go code). These types of functions are called *constructor functions*.

Using the same `point` struct that I use in the preceding section, let's define a function as follows:

```
func newPoint(x, y, z float32) *point {
    p := point{x: x, y: y, z: z}
    return &p
}
```

The `newPoint()` function accepts three arguments — x, y, and z — to assign to each field in the `point` struct, and it returns a pointer to a `point` struct (as indicated using the *). Within the function, it creates and initializes a `point` struct. Finally, it returns the address of the point struct (using the & character).

To create a new `point` struct, you can now use the `newPoint()` function like this:

```
pt4 := newPoint(7.8, 9.1, 2.3)
fmt.Println(pt4) // &{7.8 9.1 2.3}
```

When you print it out, notice that there is an & in front of the output:

```
&{7.8 9.1 2.3}
```

This is because the `newPoint()` function returns a pointer to a `point` struct. Essentially, pt4 is just pointing to the `point` struct created within the `newPoint()` function (see Figure 7-1).

TIP

To print out the values of each field in the `point` struct, you can directly use the field names and the pointer will be automatically dereferenced:

```
fmt.Println(pt4.x) // 7.8
```

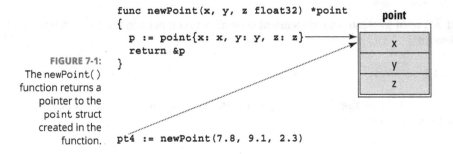

FIGURE 7-1:
The newPoint( )
function returns a
pointer to the
point struct
created in the
function.

Making a Copy of a Struct

The result from the newPoint() function (pt4 in the preceding example) is a pointer to a struct. If you try to assign pt4 to another variable — say, pt5 — then pt5 will also point to the same struct pointed to by pt4:

```
pt5 := pt4
```

Figure 7-2 shows pt5 pointing to the same struct as pt4.

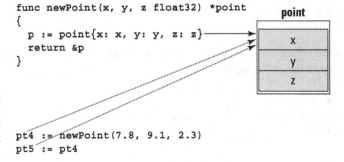

FIGURE 7-2:
Both pt4 and pt5
are pointing to
the same struct
instance.

To verify this, let's change a field in pt5 and then point out the values for both pt4 and pt5:

```
pt5.x = 0
fmt.Println(pt4) // &{0 9.1 2.3}
fmt.Println(pt5) // &{0 9.1 2.3}
```

The output shows that modifying pt5 affects the values for pt4 as well, because they're both pointing to the same struct.

If you want to create an independent copy of pt4, you need to use the * character, like this:

```
pt6 := *pt4
```

Figure 7-3 shows that pt6 is now pointing to a copy of the point struct originally pointed to by pt4.

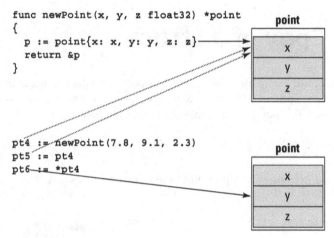

FIGURE 7-3:
pt6 is now pointing to a new instance of the point struct.

The following code snippet proves that pt4 and pt6 are now pointing to different copies of the point struct:

```
pt6.z = 0
fmt.Println(pt4) // &{7.8 9.1 2.3}
fmt.Println(pt6) // {7.8 9.1 0}
```

The key difference between pt4 and pt6 is that pt4 is a pointer to a point struct, while pt6 is a variable of type point.

If you now assign pt6 to another variable — say, pt7 — then pt7 would contain a copy of pt6:

```
pt7 := pt6
```

TIP

Struct is a value type, so when you assign one struct variable to another, a new copy of the struct is created and assigned.

If you want to create a reference to a struct — say, pt7 — you use the & prefix:

```
pt8 := &pt7
```

Figure 7-4 shows pt7 having a copy of pt6, while pt8 is pointing to the copy held by pt7.

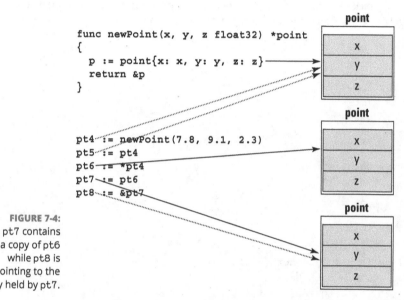

Defining Methods in Structs

You can create *methods* defined on a struct type in Go. For example, in the earlier example on the point type, you may want to calculate the distance of the point from the origin. As such, it would be really useful if you could call a method directly on a point variable, like this:

```
pt4.length()  // length() calculates the distance of the
              // point from the origin
```

REMEMBER

A method is basically a function (turn to Chapter 5 for more on functions) that has a *receiver*. For example, say you have a function named length() and it calculates the distance of a point struct from the origin. To use this function, you would call it like this:

```
length(pt4)
```

A method, on the other hand, is a function attached to a specific type. So if the `length()` function is declared to be a method, it will be called like this:

```
pt4.length()
```

Other than this, functions and methods work the same way.

To implement a method on a struct, you can define a function named `length` together with a receiver, as shown in the following code snippet:

```
package main

import (
    "fmt"
    "math"
)

type point struct {
    x float32
    y float32
    z float32
}

func (p point) length() float64 {
    return math.Sqrt(
        (math.Pow(float64(p.x), 2) +
            math.Pow(float64(p.y), 2) +
            math.Pow(float64(p.z), 2)))
}

func newPoint(x, y, z float32) *point {
    p := point{x: x, y: y, z: z}
    return &p
}
```

Notice that the `length()` method has a *value receiver* (it receives an argument of value type) of type `point`:

```
func (p point) length() float64 {
```

This means that you can call the `length()` method from a `point` struct:

```
func main() {
    pt4 := newPoint(7.8, 9.1, 2.3)
```

```
        fmt.Println(pt4.length()) // 12.2040980698644
}
```

In this example, when you call the length() method from the pt4 struct, a *copy* of the pt4 struct is passed into the length() method.

Alternatively, you can also modify the method with a *pointer receiver* (it receives an argument of pointer type), like this:

```
func (p *point) length() float64 {
```

In this case, when you call the length() method, a *reference* to the struct is passed into it instead of a copy. For calculating the distance of a point from the origin, it does not matter if you declare the method with a value or pointer receiver because you're never going to modify the value of the fields inside the struct.

Sometimes declaring a struct method with a pointer receiver is useful. Suppose you want to create a method to move a point in the coordinate space. In this case, you will modify the x-, y-, and z-coordinates, so it's useful to have a pointer receiver, like this:

```
func (p *point) move(deltax, deltay, deltaz float32) {
    p.x += deltax
    p.y += deltay
    p.z += deltaz
}
```

Because the method will receive a point struct by reference, you can directly modify the x, y, and z fields without needing to return the struct from the method.

Here's how to move a point by calling the move() function:

```
func main() {

    pt4 := newPoint(7.8, 9.1, 2.3)
    fmt.Println(pt4.length())

    pt4.move(0.1, 0.1, 0.1)
    fmt.Println(*pt4)          // {7.9 9.200001 2.3999999}
}
```

Notice that you can explicitly deference pt4 by prefixing it with the *.

Comparing Structs

You can compare two structs to see if they're equal, provided all the fields inside the struct are comparable. For example, you can compare the following structs — pt1, pt2, and pt3:

```
pt1 := point{x: 5.6, y: 3.8, z: 6.9}
pt2 := point{x: 5.6, y: 3.8, z: 6.9}
pt3 := point{x: 6.5, y: 3.8, z: 6.9}

fmt.Println(pt1 == pt2) // true
fmt.Println(pt2 == pt3) // false
```

However, suppose now the point struct contains a field (name), which is a slice of string:

```
type point struct {
    x       float32
    y       float32
    z       float32
    name []string
}
```

You can no longer compare these structs:

```
pt1 := point{x: 5.6, y: 3.8, z: 6.9,
        name: []string{"pt1"}}

pt2 := point{x: 5.6, y: 3.8, z: 6.9,
        name: []string{"pt2"}}

// invalid operation: pt1 == pt2 (struct containing
//    []string cannot be compared)
fmt.Println(pt1 == pt2)
```

TIP

You can't directly compare structs that contain fields that aren't comparable, but you *can* use the cmp package (https://pkg.go.dev/github.com/google/go-cmp/cmp) to do that. In addition, the cmp package allows you to override the Equal function so that you can implement your own custom comparer of structs.

To install the cmp package, use the following command in Terminal or Command Prompt:

```
$ go get -u github.com/google/go-cmp/cmp
```

One thing to take note of when using the cmp package is that your struct must be exported, so you need to capitalize the struct name and all its fields:

```go
type Point struct {
    X       float32
    Y       float32
    Z       float32
    Name []string
}
```

You can now compare structs as shown in the following code snippet:

```go
package main

import (
    "fmt"
    "github.com/google/go-cmp/cmp"
)

type Point struct {
    X       float32
    Y       float32
    Z       float32
    Name []string
}

func main() {
    pt1 := Point{X: 5.6, Y: 3.8, Z: 6.9,
            Name: []string{"pt1"}}
    pt2 := Point{X: 5.6, Y: 3.8, Z: 6.9,
            Name: []string{"pt"}}
    pt3 := Point{X: 5.6, Y: 3.8, Z: 6.9,
            Name: []string{"pt"}}

    fmt.Println(cmp.Equal(pt1, pt2)) // false
    fmt.Println(cmp.Equal(pt2, pt3)) // true
}
```

Notice that pt2 and pt3 are deemed to be equal because their fields all have the same values.

What if you want to implement your own custom comparer? Say you would deem two structs to be equal as long as their x, y, and z fields are equal? In this case, you can implement your own Equal() method, like this:

```go
type Point struct {
    X     float32
    Y     float32
    Z     float32
    Name []string
}

func (p1 Point) Equal(p2 Point) bool {
    if p1.X == p2.X &&
        p1.Y == p2.Y &&
        p1.Z == p2.Z {
        return true
    }
    return false
}
```

The following statement will now yield true for both comparisons:

```go
fmt.Println(cmp.Equal(pt1, pt2)) // true
fmt.Println(cmp.Equal(pt2, pt3)) // true
```

Chapter **8**

Establishing Relationships Using Maps

n earlier chapters, I fill you in on arrays and slices, where the position of items is important, and items are accessed by their locations. A map, on the other hand, is a hash table that stores data in an associative manner. Items in a map are not accessed according to their positions. Instead, you use *keys* (a set of unique value that identifies the elements in a map). Maps make adding and removing items extremely easy.

In this chapter, I show you how to work with maps in Go, create a map of structs, and sort a map based on its content.

Creating Maps in Go

A Go map type has the following syntax:

```
map[keyType] valueType
```

Here is an example of a map variable that stores a collection of int values with the key that is of the type string:

```
package main

var heights map[string]int

func main() {

}
```

Because the map type is a reference type, you need to first initialize it using the make() function before you can use it:

```
heights = make(map[string]int)
```

TIP

By default, the map variable (heights) is pointing to nil before you initialize it using the make() function.

After the map variable is initialized, you can use it. Let's add the key "Peter" to the map and assign it the value of 170 (his height in centimeters):

```
heights["Peter"] = 170
```

You can add the heights of a couple more people:

```
heights["Joan"] = 168
heights["Jan"] = 175
```

You can visualize the map as a collection of key/value pairs as shown in Figure 8-1.

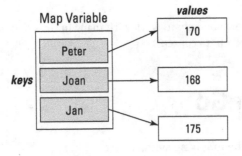

FIGURE 8-1:
The map with three key/value pairs.

TIP

How the values in a map are stored internally is dependent on implementation — it doesn't affect the way you use the map.

To retrieve the value of each key, you simply specify the key in the map, like this:

```
fmt.Println(heights["Peter"]) // 170
fmt.Println(heights["Joan"])  // 168
fmt.Println(heights["Jan"])   // 175
```

In the following sections, I show you how to

>> Initialize a map with a map literal.

>> Check for the existence of a key in a map.

>> Delete a key in a map.

>> Iterate over a map.

>> Get all the keys in a map.

>> Set the order of iteration in a map.

Initializing a map with a map literal

Apart from using the make() function to initialize a map variable, you can also initialize a map variable using a *map literal* (a set of key/value pairs):

```
heights := map[string]int{
    "Peter": 170,
    "Joan":  168,
    "Jan":   175,   // <-- note the comma here
}
```

This statement creates and initialize a map with three items.

Checking the existence of a key

In the "Creating maps in Go" section, I explain how you can retrieve the value of a key by specifying the key in the map. But what happens if the key doesn't exist in the map, as in the following example?

```
fmt.Println(heights["Jim"]) // 0
```

In this statement, because "Jim" is not an existing key in the map variable, the result would be 0, the value's zero-value. Although this information is helpful, it doesn't really tell you whether the specified key exists or whether the actual value of this key is 0.

TIP

A better way to get the value of a key would be to use a two-value assignment test to check for the key's existence:

```
if v, ok := heights["Jim"]; ok {
    fmt.Println(v)
} else {
    fmt.Println("Key does not exist")
}
```

In this example, retrieving the value of "Jim" from the heights variable returns two values: the value of the specified key, as well as a Boolean value (stored in ok) indicating if the operation succeeded. If ok is true, the specified key exists, and you can go ahead and use its value (stored in v). If ok is false, the key does not exist.

Deleting a key

To delete a key from a map, you use the delete() function, with the following syntax:

```
delete(map, key)
```

The delete() function does not return a value after deleting the specified key, and it won't inform you if the specified key doesn't exist in the map variable. So, it's useful to check for the key's existence before you delete it:

```
if _, ok := heights["Joan"]; ok {
    delete(heights, "Joan")
} else {
    fmt.Println("Key does not exist")
}
```

Getting the number of items in a map

To get the number of items in the map, use the len() function:

```
fmt.Println(len(heights))
```

For an uninitialized map, the `len()` function will return zero:

```
var weights map[string]int
fmt.Println(len(weights)) // 0
```

Iterating over a map

To iterate over a map variable, you can use the `for-range` loop:

```
for k, v := range heights {
    fmt.Println(k, v)
}
```

In this code snippet, k represents the key and v represents the value of each item in the map. The preceding statement produces the following output:

```
Peter 170
Joan 168
Jan 175
```

REMEMBER

The order of the output isn't guaranteed to be the same each time the code is run. This is because items in the map variable are not ordered. If you need to print the items is a particular order, you need to sort them yourself (more on this in the "Setting the iteration order in a map" and "Sorting the items in a map by values" sections).

Getting all the keys in a map

To get all the keys in the map, use a `for-range` loop and store the keys into a slice:

```
// get all the keys in map
var keys []string
for k := range heights {
    keys = append(keys, k)
}
fmt.Println(keys) // [Jan Peter Joan]
```

The preceding code snippet appends all the keys in the `heights` map variable into the slice named `keys`.

REMEMBER

The order of the keys retrieved is not guaranteed.

Setting the iteration order in a map

Earlier, I show you that when you print out the items in a map, all the items are not guaranteed to be printed in a specific order. So, if you need to, say, print all the keys in alphabetical order, you have to sort the keys first (using the sort package):

```go
import (
    "fmt"
    "sort"
)
...


    sort.Strings(keys)
    fmt.Println(keys) // [Jan Joan Peter]
```

After the keys are sorted, you can then use the for-range loop to iterate over the keys and print out the value of each key:

```go
for _, k := range keys {
    fmt.Println(k, heights[k])
}
```

This way, the order of the key and its associated value is guaranteed.

Sorting the items in a map by values

If you want to sort the order of items in a map based on the values, things will get a little involved. Using the existing example where you have three items in the map:

```go
heights := make(map[string]int)
heights["Peter"] = 170
heights["Joan"] = 168
heights["Jan"] = 175
```

Suppose you want to now print out the names of all the people in the map based on their height — from the shortest to the tallest. To do that, you need to first define a struct, followed by a slice:

```go
package main

import (
    "fmt"
)
```

```
type kv struct {
    key    string
    value int
}

type kvPairs []kv

var heights map[string]int
```

Now create a slice called p and set it to the same length as that of heights. After that, add each key/value pair in the heights map as a struct into the slice:

```
func main() {
    heights := make(map[string]int)
    heights["Peter"] = 170
    heights["Joan"] = 168
    heights["Jan"] = 175

    p := make(kvPairs, len(heights))
    i := 0
    for k, v := range heights {
        p[i] = kv{k, v}
        i++
    }
}
```

Figure 8-2 shows how p looks now.

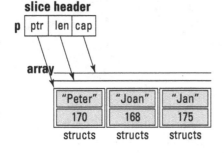

FIGURE 8-2:
All the items in the map have been added as structs into the slice p.

When you now print out p, like this:

```
fmt.Println(p)
```

You should see the following:

```
[{Peter 170} {Joan 168} {Jan 175}]
```

The next step would be to sort the p slice, using the Sort() function from the sort package. However, before you use the Sort() function, you need to implement the Sort interface:

>> Len(): Returns the length of the collection.

>> Less(): Receives two integers that will serve as indices from the collection, and you define how the items should be sorted.

>> Swap(): Implements the change needed after the Less method is called.

TIP Chapter 10 covers interfaces in more detail.

Implementing these three functions would allow the Sort() function to sort the kvPairs slice according to your sort criteria:

```go
package main

import (
    "fmt"
    "sort"
)

type kv struct {
    key     string
    value int
}

type kvPairs []kv

var heights map[string]int

func (p kvPairs) Len() int {
    // returns the length of the collection
    return len(p)
}

func (p kvPairs) Less(i, j int) bool {
    // indicates the first value (height) must be smaller
    // than the second value
    return p[i].value < p[j].value
}
```

```
func (p kvPairs) Swap(i, j int) {
    // swaps the items in the collection
    p[i], p[j] = p[j], p[i]
}
```

In the preceding code snippets, the kvPairs slice implements the three methods so that the items' values within the slice can be sorted in ascending order.

You can now finally sort the p slice and print out the items based on the heights of the three people (from shortest to tallest):

```
sort.Sort(p)

fmt.Println(p)
// [{Joan 168} {Peter 170} {Jan 175}]

for _, v := range p {
    fmt.Println(v)
}
/*
    {Joan 168}
    {Peter 170}
    {Jan 175}
*/
```

Using Structs and Maps in Go

In the previous sections, I show you how to create a map using Go's basic data types. In reality, when dealing with more complicated data, you often use maps together with structs. In the following sections, I show you how to create a map of structs, as well as how to convert a map into a slice so that you can perform your own custom sorting.

Creating a map of structs

Suppose you have people and dob structs defined as follows:

```
type dob struct {
    day   int
    month int
    year  int
}
```

```
type people struct {
    name   string
    email string
    dob    dob
}
```

To store a collection of `people` struct, you can declare a map of `int` key and value of type `people`:

```
var members map[int]people
```

The following code snippet shows how to initialize the `members` map:

```
package main

import "fmt"

type dob struct {
    day   int
    month int
    year  int
}

type people struct {
    name   string
    email string
    dob    dob
}

var members map[int]people

func main() {
    members = make(map[int]people)

    members[1] = people{
        name:  "Mary Smith",
        email: "marysmith@example.com",
        dob: dob{
            day:   17,
            month: 3,
            year:  1990,
        },
    }
```

```
    members[2] = people{
        name:  "John Smith",
        email: "johnsmith@example.com",
        dob: dob{
            day:   9,
            month: 12,
            year:  1988,
        },
    }
    members[3] = people{
        name:  "Janet Doe",
        email: "janetdoe@example.com",
        dob: dob{
            day:   1,
            month: 12,
            year:  1988,
        },
    }
    members[4] = people{
        name:  "Adam Jones",
        email: "adamjones@example.com",
        dob: dob{
            day:   19,
            month: 8,
            year:  2001,
        },
    }
}
```

To print out all the members, you can use the `for-range` loop:

```
for k, v := range members {
    fmt.Println(k, v.name, v.email, v.dob)
}
```

You may get an output like this:

```
2 John Smith johnsmith@example.com {9 12 1988}
3 Janet Doe janetdoe@example.com {1 12 1988}
4 Adam Jones adamjones@example.com {19 8 2001}
1 Mary Smith marysmith@example.com {17 3 1990}
```

Sorting a map of structs

Because a map can store data of different types — *primitive types* (basic data types available within the Go language), as well as *structured types* (types that are composed of other data types) — there are no built-in functions to easily custom-sort a map based on its content.

But what if you need to print out the content of a map based on a specific order? You could first copy out all the items in the members map into a slice of people:

```
// get all the keys in members
var keys []int
for k := range members {
    keys = append(keys, k)
}

// sort the keys in ascending order
sort.Ints(keys)

// copy the value in members to the slice
var sliceMembers []people
for _, k := range keys {
    sliceMembers = append(sliceMembers, members[k])
}
```

In the preceding code snippet, you first extract the keys in the members map and then sort them in ascending order before you copy the value of each key into the slice. The sliceMembers is now a slice of the people struct. Let's print it out to see its content (formatted for clarity):

```
[
    {Mary Smith marysmith@example.com {17 3 1990}}
    {John Smith johnsmith@example.com {9 12 1988}}
    {Janet Doe janetdoe@example.com {1 12 1988}}
    {Adam Jones adamjones@example.com {19 8 2001}}
]
```

To sort a slice, you can use the SliceStable() function from the sort package. The SliceStable() function has the following signature:

```
func SliceStable(slice interface{},
                 less func(i, j int) bool)
```

It takes in a slice as the first argument and an anonymous function as the second argument. The anonymous function has two parameters and returns a `bool` value. The parameters i and j represent the index of the items in the slice to compare. The return value of this anonymous function indicates if the two items in the slice are in the correct order (which is determined by you as to how the items are to be sorted).

So, if you want to sort all the members in the `sliceMembers` based on their date-of-birth (dob) from oldest to youngest, you can call the `SliceStable()` function as follows:

```
sort.SliceStable(sliceMembers, func(i, j int) bool {
    // compare year
    if sliceMembers[i].dob.year !=
        sliceMembers[j].dob.year {
        return sliceMembers[i].dob.year <
                sliceMembers[j].dob.year
    }

    // compare month
    if sliceMembers[i].dob.month !=
        sliceMembers[j].dob.month {
        return sliceMembers[i].dob.month <
                sliceMembers[j].dob.month
    }

    // compare day
    return sliceMembers[i].dob.day <
            sliceMembers[j].dob.day
})

for _, v := range sliceMembers {
    fmt.Println(v.name, v.email, v.dob)
}
```

Here's how you ensure that the age of the members is sorted in descending order:

1. **Check the year of the two members.**

    If they are not the same, check if the year of member i is less than the year of member j. If the year of member i is less than member j, this means the order of the member is in correct order (a person is older than another if his year of birth is smaller than the other one) and the function returns a true. Otherwise, the `SliceStable()` function will automatically swap the two members.

2. **If the years of the two members are the same, check the months.**

Again, if the months are not the same, you compare the months of the two members. If the comparison returns a false, the SliceStable() function will swap the two members.

3. **If the year and month of the two members are the same, compare the day of the two members.**

Return a true if the day of member i is smaller than the day of member j.

At the end of the swapping, the sliceMembers will now have its items sorted according to date of birth. You can verify this by printings its content:

```
for _, v := range sliceMembers {
    fmt.Println(v.name, v.email, v.dob)
}
```

You should see the following output:

```
Janet Doe janetdoe@example.com {1 12 1988}
John Smith johnsmith@example.com {9 12 1988}
Mary Smith marysmith@example.com {17 3 1990}
Adam Jones adamjones@example.com {19 8 2001}
```

What if you just want to sort the members based on their year? In this case, you simply need to perform the comparison for the year in the SliceStable() function:

```
sort.SliceStable(sliceMembers, func(i, j int) bool {
    return sliceMembers[i].dob.year <
            sliceMembers[j].dob.year
})
```

You should now see the following output:

```
John Smith johnsmith@example.com {9 12 1988}
Janet Doe janetdoe@example.com {1 12 1988}
Mary Smith marysmith@example.com {17 3 1990}
Adam Jones adamjones@example.com {19 8 2001}
```

TIP The SliceStable() function has a cousin function that is very similar: Slice(). Both these two functions allow you to sort a slice, but the Slice() function doesn't guarantee the sort result to be stable. What does that mean? If you use the Slice() function to sort based on the person's year of birth, like this:

```
sort.Slice(sliceMembers, func(i, j int) bool {
    return sliceMembers[i].dob.year <
            sliceMembers[j].dob.year
})
```

The result may look like this:

```
John Smith johnsmith@example.com {9 12 1988}
Janet Doe janetdoe@example.com {1 12 1988}
Mary Smith marysmith@example.com {17 3 1990}
Adam Jones adamjones@example.com {19 8 2001}
```

Or it may look like this:

```
Janet Doe janetdoe@example.com {1 12 1988}
John Smith johnsmith@example.com {9 12 1988}
Mary Smith marysmith@example.com {17 3 1990}
Adam Jones adamjones@example.com {19 8 2001}
```

See the difference? Because both John and Janet have the same year of birth, the Slice() function doesn't guarantee that the result after sorting follows the original order, where John comes before Janet (check the output of the sliceMembers to confirm this).

TECHNICAL
STUFF

In programming, *stable* sorting algorithms preserve the relative order of equal items, while *unstable* sorting algorithms do not. In other words, after the sorting, a stable sorting algorithm will always preserve the original order of two equal items. The SliceStable() function sorts your slices using a stable sorting algorithm, while the Slice() function does not.

REMEMBER

If the order of the original elements is important, you should always use the SliceStable() function for sorting slices.

Chapter **9**

Encoding and Decoding Data Using JSON

JavaScript Object Notation (JSON) is a standard, text-based format for representing data using the JavaScript object syntax. It's a lightweight and easy-to-parse data representation language, commonly used for communicating between web servers and clients.

In this chapter, I explain the basics of JSON and how you can manipulate JSON content in your Go applications.

Getting Acquainted with JSON

JSON is growing more and more popular these days. It's commonly used in data representation, as well as data exchange. JSON is less verbose than XML, but that's exactly what makes it so useful. JSON strings are shorter than their XML equivalents, and parsing JSON strings is a walk in the park.

TECHNICAL STUFF

If you aren't familiar with XML, check out the introduction to XML at www.w3schools.com/xml/xml:whatis.asp.

In this section, I give you a brief walk-through of JSON. If you're already super-familiar with JSON, you can skip directly to the "Decoding JSON" section. But even if you already have some experience dealing with JSON, I recommend at least glancing through this section.

JSON supports the following data types:

>> Object

>> String

>> Boolean

>> Number

>> Array

>> null

The following sections elaborate on each of these data types.

TIP

If you want even more information on JSON, check out *Coding with JavaScript For Dummies,* by Chris Minnick and Eva Holland (Wiley).

Object

An *Object* is an unordered collection of key/value pairs enclosed in a pair of curly braces ({}). The following is an example of an empty object:

```
{}
```

String

A *String* is a sequence of characters. The *key* in an object must be a String, while the *value* can be a String, a Boolean, a Number, an Array, null, or another Object.

The following shows an Object with one key/value pair:

```
{
    "firstName": "John"
}
```

An object can have multiple key/value pairs, like this:

```
{
    "firstName": "John",
    "lastName": "Doe"
}
```

TIP

Note that there's a comma (,) after John, essentially separating the first key/value pair and the second.

Each key in the Object must be unique. For example, the following example is *not* a valid JSON string because you have two key/value pairs having the same key (firstName):

```
{
    "firstName": "John",
    "firstName": "Doe"
}
```

Boolean

A Boolean value can either be true or false:

```
{
    "firstName": "John",
    "lastName": "Doe",
    "isMember": true
}
```

Number

A Number value can either be an *integer* (whole number) or a *floating-point number* (decimal-point number):

```
{
    "firstName": "John",
    "lastName": "Doe",
    "isMember": true,
    "weight": 79.5,
    "height": 1.73,
    "children": 3
}
```

Object

The value of a key can also be another Object, as the following example shows:

```
{
    "firstName": "John",
    "lastName": "Doe",
    "isMember": true,
    "weight": 79.5,
    "height": 1.73,
    "children": 3,
    "address": {
        "line1": "123 Street",
        "line2": "San Francisco",
        "state": "CA",
        "postal": "12345"
    }
}
```

Array

An *Array* is an ordered sequence of Objects:

```
{
    "firstName": "John",
    "lastName": "Doe",
    "isMember": true,
    "weight": 79.5,
    "height": 1.73,
    "children": 3,
    "address": {
        "line1": "123 Street",
        "line2": "San Francisco",
        "state": "CA",
        "postal": "12345"
    },
    "phone": [
        {
            "type": "work",
            "number": "1234567"
        },
```

```
      {
          "type": "home",
          "number": "8765432"
      },
      {

          "type": "mobile",
          "number": "1234876"
      }
   ]
}
```

Note that Arrays are denoted with a pair of brackets ([ ]).

null

When a key has no value, you can assign a null to it:

```
{
    "firstName": "John",
    "lastName": "Doe",
    "isMember": true,
    "weight": 79.5,
    "height": 1.73,
    "children": 3,
    "address": {
        "line1": "123 Street",
        "line2": "San Francisco",
        "state": "CA",
        "postal": "12345"
    },
    "phone": [
        {
            "type": "work",
            "number": "1234567"
        },
        {
            "type": "home",
            "number": "8765432"
        },
```

```
        {
            "type": "mobile",
            "number": "1234876"
        }
    ],
    "oldMembershipNo": null
}
```

TIP

A good online tool that I often use to check if a string is a valid JSON string is
`https://jsonlint.com/`. Enter your JSON string into the website (see Figure 9-1),
click the Validate JSON button, and you're immediately told whether your JSON
string is valid.

FIGURE 9-1:
Using JSONLint
to validate a
JSON string.

Decoding JSON

When you know how a JSON string looks (see the "Getting Acquainted with JSON"
section, earlier in this chapter), you need to know how to decode it to a form that
you can work with in Go. In the following sections, I show you how to decode JSON

to a struct and to an array, how to decode embedded objects in JSON, how to map custom attribute names in JSON to a struct, and how to decode an unstructured JSON string.

Decoding JSON to a struct

Let's start off with the most straightforward way to convert a JSON string to a Go struct. Say you have the following JSON string:

```
{
    "firstname" : "Wei-Meng",
    "lastname"  : "Lee"
}
```

And you want to decode this JSON string to a struct in Go. For this, you use the encoding/json package in Go, like this:

```
package main

import (
    "encoding/json"
    "fmt"
)
```

Next, you define a struct in Go so that the JSON string can map onto it:

```
type People struct {
    Firstname string
    Lastname  string
}
```

In the preceding code snippet, I created a struct named People with two fields: Firstname and Lastname. You can name the struct anything you want, but the fields in the struct must match that of the keys in the JSON string.

Finally, you create a variable of type People and then use the json.Unmarshal() function to decode the JSON string:

```
func main() {
    var person People

    jsonString := `{"firstname":"Wei-Meng",
                    "lastname":"Lee"}`
```

```
    err := json.Unmarshal([]byte(jsonString), &person)
    if err == nil {
        fmt.Println(person.Firstname)
        fmt.Println(person.Lastname)
    } else {
        fmt.Println(err)
    }
}
```

The json.Unmarshal() function parses the JSON-encoded data (you need to con-vert the JSON string to a byte slice) and stores the result into person. (You need to pass in the address of person using the & address operator.)

If the unmarshalling (decoding) works, the json.Unmarshal() function returns a nil, and you can now find the value stored in the person variable.

REMEMBER

Be sure to capitalize the first character of each field in the People struct. If the field name starts with a lowercase letter, it won't be exported beyond the current package, and the fields won't be visible to the json.Unmarshal() function.

The previous code snippet prints out the following output:

```
Wei-Meng
Lee
```

Decoding JSON to arrays

Often, your JSON string may contain arrays of objects, as shown in the following example:

```
[
    {
        "firstname":"Wei-Meng",
        "lastname":"Lee"
    },
    {
        "firstname":"Mickey",
        "lastname":"Mouse"
    }
]
```

In this case, you can simply create an array of the People struct and pass it to the json.Unmarshal() function, like this:

```
func main() {
    var persons []People
    jsonString :=
        `[
            {
                "firstname":"Wei-Meng",
                "lastname":"Lee"
            },
            {
                "firstname":"Mickey",
                "lastname":"Mouse"
            }
        ]`

    json.Unmarshal([]byte(jsonString), &persons)

    for _, person := range persons {
        fmt.Println(person.Firstname)
        fmt.Println(person.Lastname)
    }
}
```

You then use a for loop to iterate through the array of the People struct. The output now looks like this:

```
Wei-Meng
Lee
Mickey
Mouse
```

Decoding embedded objects

Sometimes your JSON string may contain nested objects, as shown in the following example:

```
[
    {
        "firstname":"Wei-Meng",
        "lastname":"Lee",
        "details": {
            "height":175,
            "weight":70.0
        }
    },
```

```
    {
        "firstname":"Mickey",
        "lastname":"Mouse",
        "details": {
            "height":105,
            "weight":85.5
        }
    }
]
```

The value of the details key is another JSON object. To decode it, you can add another member called Details to the People struct, like this:

```
type People struct {
    Firstname string
    Lastname  string
    Details   struct {
        Height int
        Weight float32
    }
}
```

And you can now decode it as usual:

```
package main

import (
    "encoding/json"
    "fmt"
)

type People struct {
    Firstname string
    Lastname  string
    Details   struct {
        Height int
        Weight float32
    }
}

func main() {
    var persons []People
    jsonString :=
        `[
```

```
            {
                "firstname":"Wei-Meng",
                "lastname":"Lee",
                "details": {
                    "height":175,
                    "weight":70.0
                }
            },
            {
                "firstname":"Mickey",
                "lastname":"Mouse",
                "details": {
                    "height":105,
                    "weight":85.5
                }
            }
        ]`

    json.Unmarshal([]byte(jsonString), &persons)

    for _, person := range persons {
        fmt.Println(person.Firstname)
        fmt.Println(person.Lastname)
        fmt.Println(person.Details.Height)
        fmt.Println(person.Details.Weight)
    }
}
```

The output looks like this:

```
Wei-Meng
Lee
175
70
Mickey
Mouse
105
85.5
```

Mapping custom attribute names

Sometimes the keys in your JSON string can't be mapped directly to members of your struct in Go. Consider the following example:

```
{
    "base currency":"EUR",
    "destination currency":"USD"
}
```

Notice that the keys in this JSON string have spaces in them. If you try to map it directly to a struct, you'll run into problems because variable names in Go can't have spaces. To resolve this issue, you can make use of *struct field tags* (string literals placed after each field in a struct), like this:

```
type Rates struct {
    Base   string `json:"base currency"`
    Symbol string `json:"destination currency"`
}
```

Here, you're explicitly specifying which JSON key to map to which member in the struct:

» "base currency" maps to Base

» "destination currency" maps to Symbol

So, you can now decode the JSON string as follows:

```
package main

import (
    "encoding/json"
    "fmt"
)

type Rates struct {
    Base   string `json:"base currency"`
    Symbol string `json:"destination currency"`
}

func main() {
    jsonString :=
```

```
    `{
        "base currency":"EUR",
        "destination currency":"USD"
    }`

    var rates Rates
    json.Unmarshal([]byte(jsonString), &rates)
    fmt.Println(rates.Base)    // EUR
    fmt.Println(rates.Symbol) // USD
}
```

Mapping unstructured data

The previous few sections have shown relatively simple JSON strings. In the real world, though, the JSON strings that you'll manipulate are often large and unstructured. Plus, you may only need to retrieve specific values from the JSON string.

Consider the following JSON string:

```
{
    "success": true,
    "timestamp": 1588779306,
    "base": "EUR",
    "date": "2020-05-06",
    "rates": {
        "AUD": 1.683349,
        "CAD": 1.528643,
        "GBP": 0.874757,
        "SGD": 1.534513,
        "USD": 1.080054
    }
}
```

Suppose you only want to extract the value for SGD (Singapore dollars). In this case, instead of defining an entire structure, you'll define the following:

```
var result map[string]interface{}
```

The preceding statement creates a variable named result of type map, whose key is of type string, and each corresponding value is of type interface{}. This empty interface indicates that the value can be of any type.

To decode the JSON string, you pass in the address of `result` into the `json.Unmarshal()` function, like this:

```
json.Unmarshal([]byte(jsonString), &result)
```

After the JSON string has been decoded, try to extract the value of the "success" key. Pass "success" as the key to the `result` map variable:

```
fmt.Println(result["success"])  // true
```

To extract the value of the "rates" key, you pass "rates" as the key to the `result` map variable:

```
rates := result["rates"]
fmt.Println(rates)
```

The type of `rates` is `map[string] interface{}` (see Figure 9-2), which means its value could be of any type — a `map`, a `string`, or an `int`. When you print out the value of `rates`, you get the following:

```
map[AUD:1.683349 CAD:1.528643 GBP:0.874757
    SGD:1.534513 USD:1.080054]
```

rates

```
map[string] interface{}
```

Key (string)

```
"rates": Value (interface{})
      {
          "AUD": 1.683349,
          "CAD": 1.528643,
          "GBP": 0.874757,
          "SGD": 1.534513,
          "USD": 1.080054
      }
```

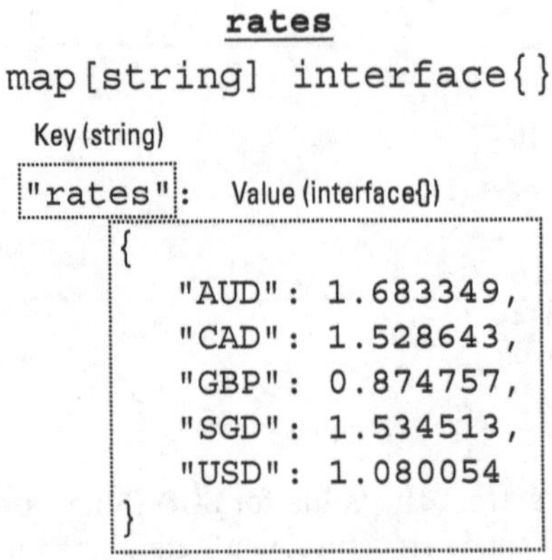

FIGURE 9-2: Examining the type of rates, which is `map[string] interface{}`.

To get the value of SGD, you first need to assert `rates` to a `map` type with expected key/value types (see Figure 9-3):

```
currencies := rates.(map[string]interface{})
```

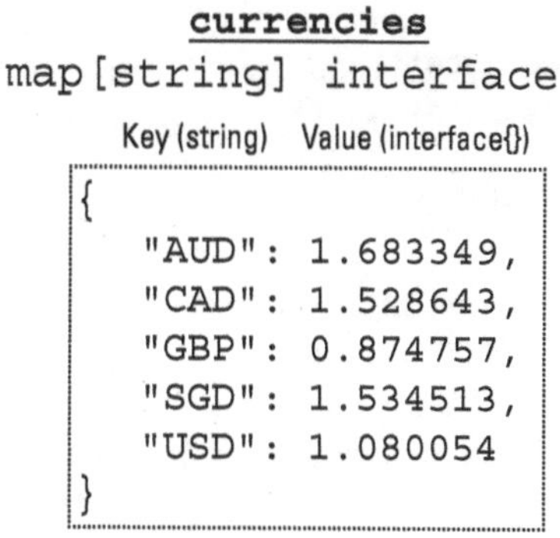

currencies

```
map[string] interface{}
```

Key (string)   Value (interface{})

```
{
    "AUD": 1.683349,
    "CAD": 1.528643,
    "GBP": 0.874757,
    "SGD": 1.534513,
    "USD": 1.080054
}
```

FIGURE 9-3:
Asserting the
value of rates to
the type
map[string]
interface{}.

Finally, you can now extract the value of SGD:

```
SGD := currencies["SGD"]
fmt.Println(SGD)    // 1.534513
```

The complete code for this section is as follows:

```go
package main

import (
    "encoding/json"
    "fmt"
)

func main() {
    jsonString :=
        `{
            "success": true,
            "timestamp": 1588779306,
            "base": "EUR",
            "date": "2020-05-06",
            "rates": {
                "AUD": 1.683349,
                "CAD": 1.528643,
                "GBP": 0.874757,
                "SGD": 1.534513,
                "USD": 1.080054
            }
        }`

    var result map[string]interface{}
```

```
    json.Unmarshal([]byte(jsonString), &result)
    fmt.Println(result["success"]) // true

    rates := result["rates"]
    fmt.Println(rates)
    // map[USD:1.080054 AUD:1.683349 CAD:1.528643
    //      GBP:0.874757 SGD:1.534513]

    currencies := rates.(map[string]interface{})
    SGD := currencies["SGD"]
    fmt.Println(SGD)
    // 1.534513
}
```

The following statement indicates that result is a variable of type map, with key of type string, and value of type interface (which can be of any type):

```
var result map[string] interface{}
```

The following statement asserts the rates variable as a map type with key of type string and value of type interface:

```
rates.(map[string] interface{})
```

Encoding JSON

Decoding a JSON string is useful when you receive a result from web services calls. But often the reverse is also true: You need to send your data to a web service as a JSON string. In this section, I show you how to encode your data from a struct to JSON.

Encoding structs to JSON

Let me define some structs:

```
type Name struct {
    FirstName string
    LastName  string
}
```

```
type Address struct {
    Line1 string
    Line2 string
    Line3 string
}


type Customer struct {
    Name    Name
    Email   string
    Address Address
    DOB     time.Time
}
```

Figure 9-4 shows how these structs are used together to store a customer's information.

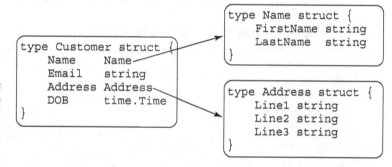

Let's now store a customer's information using the Customer struct:

```
layoutISO := "2006-01-02"
dob, _ := time.Parse(layoutISO, "2010-01-18")


john := Customer{
        Name: Name{ FirstName: "John",
                    LastName: "Smith" },
        Email: "johnsmith@example.com",
        Address: Address{
            Line1: "The White House",
            Line2: "1600 Pennsylvania Avenue NW",
            Line3: "Washington, DC 20500"
        },
        DOB: dob,
    }
```

To encode the Customer struct into JSON, you use the json.Marshal() function from the encoding/json package:

```
johnJSON, err := json.Marshal(john)
if err == nil {
    fmt.Println(string(johnJSON))
} else {
    fmt.Println(err)
}
```

The Marshal() function returns the encoded JSON (in a slice of bytes) and error (if any). You can then print out the JSON string:

```
{"Name":{"FirstName":"John","LastName":"Smith"},"Email":
"johnsmith@example.com","Address":{"Line1":"The White
House","Line2":"1600 Pennsylvania Avenue NW","Line3":
"Washington, DC 20500"},"DOB":"2010-01-18T00:00:00Z"}
```

The complete program for this section is as follows:

```
package main

import (
    "encoding/json"
    "fmt"
    "time"
)

type Name struct {
    FirstName string
    LastName  string
}

type Address struct {
    Line1 string
    Line2 string
    Line3 string
}

type Customer struct {
    Name    Name
    Email   string
    Address Address
    DOB     time.Time
}
```

```go
func main() {

    layoutISO := "2006-01-02"
    dob, _ := time.Parse(layoutISO, "2010-01-18")

    john := Customer{
            Name: Name{ FirstName: "John",
                        LastName: "Smith",
                    },
            Email: "johnsmith@example.com",
            Address: Address{
                Line1: "The White House",
                Line2: "1600 Pennsylvania Avenue NW",
                Line3: "Washington, DC 20500",
            },
            DOB: dob,
    }

    johnJSON, err := json.Marshal(john)
    if err == nil {
        fmt.Println(string(johnJSON))
    } else {
        fmt.Println(err)
    }
}
```

TIP

When you looked at the JSON output, you may have noticed that there is no indentation. If you want to indent the output and format it nicely, you can use the `json.MarshalIndent()` function:

```go
johnJSON, err := json.MarshalIndent(john, "", "    ")
```

The second argument specifies the string to prefix to the beginning of each line of output, and the third argument specifies the string to indent for each line. The preceding statement generates the following output:

```
{
    "Name": {
        "FirstName": "John",
        "LastName": "Smith"
    },
    "Email": "johnsmith@example.com",
    "Address": {
        "Line1": "The White House",
```

```
        "Line2": "1600 Pennsylvania Avenue NW",
        "Line3": "Washington, DC 20500"
    },
    "DOB": "2010-01-18T00:00:00Z"
}
```

Encoding interfaces to JSON

Sometimes you don't really want to fix the number of fields in your structs. Instead, you want to be able to add additional data as and when you need to. You can do that using empty interfaces, as in the following example:

```
type Customer map[string]interface{}
type Name map[string]interface{}
type Address map[string]interface{}
```

Using the empty interfaces, you can now create your own Customer variable and add the fields that you need, like this:

```
john := Customer{
        "Name": Name{
            "FirstName": "John",
            "LastName": "Smith",
        },
        "Email": "johnsmith@example.com",
        "Address": Address{
            "Line1": "The White House",
            "Line2": "1600 Pennsylvania Avenue NW",
            "Line3": "Washington, DC 20500",
        },
        "DOB":    dob,
    }
```

You can now use the same json.MarshalIndent() function to encode the JSON string.

The complete program for this example is as follows:

```
package main

import (
    "encoding/json"
```

```go
    "fmt"
    "time"
)
type Customer map[string]interface{}
type Name map[string]interface{}
type Address map[string]interface{}

func main() {
    layoutISO := "2006-01-02"
    dob, _ := time.Parse(layoutISO, "2010-01-18")

    john := Customer{
            "Name": Name{
                    "FirstName": "John",
                    "LastName": "Smith",
            },
            "Email": "johnsmith@example.com",
            "Address": Address{
                "Line1": "The White House",
                "Line2": "1600 Pennsylvania Avenue NW",
                "Line3": "Washington, DC 20500",
            },
            "DOB":        dob,
        }

    johnJSON, err := json.MarshalIndent(john, "", "    ")
    if err == nil {
        fmt.Println(string(johnJSON))
    } else {
        fmt.Println(err)
    }
}
```

The output is similar to the previous example.

```json
{
    "Address": {
        "Line1": "The White House",
        "Line2": "1600 Pennsylvania Avenue NW",
        "Line3": "Washington, DC 20500"
    },
```

```
    "DOB": "2010-01-18T00:00:00Z",
    "Email": "johnsmith@example.com",
    "Name": {
        "FirstName": "John",
        "LastName": "Smith"
    }
}
```

REMEMBER

The order of the keys in the output JSON is sorted alphabetically.

Chapter **10**

Defining Method Signatures Using Interfaces

E arlier in this book, I explain structs and how you can define methods in them. Another important topic in Go that is often not easy to grasp is that of interfaces. An *interface* defines the behavior of an object, specifying the methods that it needs to implement.

Interfaces serve two important purposes in Go:

» They make your code more versatile.

» They force you to adopt *code encapsulation* (the practice of hiding the implementation of your methods).

In this chapter, I explain what an interface is in Go and show you how to use it in your program. To make this topic less abstract, I illustrate interfaces with a few concrete examples.

Working with Interfaces in Go

An interface is an abstract type. It describes all the methods that a type can implement. But it only provides the method signatures, leaving the implementation entirely to the implementing type. So, you can say that interface *defines*, and doesn't *declare*, the behavior of an object of a specific type.

You may still feel a bit fuzzy on interfaces, but stick with me, and I'll show you some concrete examples.

Defining an interface

Let's first start by defining an interface type called DigitsCounter:

```
package main

import (
    "fmt"
)

type DigitsCounter interface {
}

func main() {

}
```

At this moment, the DigitsCounter interface is empty, so it isn't of much use. So, let's now add in a method to this interface:

```
type DigitsCounter interface {
    CountOddEven() (int, int)
}
```

At this point, the DigitsCounter interface has one method signature named CountOddEven(), which returns two results, both of type int. Notice that there is no implementation for the method — only the method name; input parameters, if any (there are none for this example); and the return types.

From now on, any type that implements the CountOddEven() method will also implement the DigitsCounter interface.

TIP

An interface isn't limited to one method signature; you can have as many method signatures as required.

Implementing an interface

Let's now define a custom type (using the `type` keyword) and call it `DigitString`. Declare this type to be of type `string`:

```go
package main

import (
    "fmt"
)

type DigitsCounter interface {
    CountOddEven() (int, int)
}

type DigitString string

func main() {
}
```

You now want the `DigitString` to implement the `DigitsCounter` interface, so you do this:

```go
type DigitString string

// DigitString implements DigitsCounter
func (ds DigitString) CountOddEven() (int, int) {

}
```

TIP

In Go, interfaces are implemented implicitly — you don't need to specify any "implements" keywords the way you do in some languages, such as Java.

The previous statements indicate that `DigitString` implements the `DigitsCounter` interface, and you're also providing the implementation for the `CountOddEven()` method (as defined in the `DigitsCounter` interface).

So, let's now provide the actual implementation for the CountOddEven() method:

```
func (ds DigitString) CountOddEven() (int, int) {
    odds, evens := 0, 0
    for _, digit := range ds {
        if digit%2 == 0 {
            evens++
        } else {
            odds++
        }
    }
    return odds, evens
}
```

You basically go through each of the digits in the string, count the number of odd and even digits in it, and then return the results.

Finally, you can now create a variable of type DigitString and call its CountOddEven() method:

```
func main() {
    s := DigitString("123456789")
    fmt.Println(s.CountOddEven())  // 5 4
}
```

Because DigitsCounter is a type in itself, you can also create a variable of type DigitsCounter and then assign the variable s to it:

```
var d DigitsCounter
d = s
fmt.Println(d.CountOddEven())  // 5 4
```

Looking at How You May Use Interfaces

The previous section shows how to declare an interface and how to create a type that implements it. But it doesn't really provide a compelling reason why interfaces are useful.

Suppose you're working with two different kinds of shape objects — Circle and Square. To represent these two types of objects, you have the following type declarations:

```
type Circle struct {
    radius float64
    name   string
}

type Square struct {
    length float64
    name   string
}
```

You also need to calculate the areas of these types of shapes. These two shapes have different formulas for calculating areas, so this is an excellent opportunity to make use of an interface. Declare an interface called Shape with the Area() method signature:

```
type Shape interface {
    Area() float64
}
```

To calculate the area for the Circle struct, you implement the Area() method, thereby implementing the Shape interface:

```
// Circle implements Shape
func (c Circle) Area() float64 {
    return math.Pi * math.Pow(c.radius, 2)
}
```

Likewise, you do the same for the Square struct:

```
// Square implements Shape
func (s Square) Area() float64 {
    return math.Pow(s.length, 2)
}
```

In these code snippets, both the Square and Circle types provided their own implementations for the Area() function.

Now imagine you have a number of shapes — circles and squares:

```
func main() {
    c1 := Circle{radius: 5, name: "c1"}
    s1 := Square{length: 6, name: "s1"}
}
```

To calculate the area of each shape, you could call the `Area()` method of each shape:

```
fmt.Println(c1.Area())
fmt.Println(s1.Area())
```

But this is too tedious. Because each shape implements the Shape interface, they all have the `Area()` method. So, instead of calling the `Area()` method of each shape, you can write a function to take in a slice of Shape objects and then call the `Area()` method of each object directly:

```
func calculateArea(listOfShapes []Shape) {
    for _, shape := range listOfShapes {
        fmt.Println("Area of shape is ", shape.Area())
    }
}

func main() {
    c1 := Circle{radius: 5, name: "c1"}
    s1 := Square{length: 6, name: "s1"}

    shapes := []Shape{c1, s1}
    calculateArea(shapes)
}
```

The preceding prints out the following:

```
Area of shape is   78.53981633974483
Area of shape is   36
```

Here's the complete program:

```
package main

import "fmt"

type Shape interface {
    Area() float64
}

type Circle struct {
    radius float64
}
```

```go
type Square struct {
    length float64
}

// Circle implements Shape
func (c Circle) Area() float64 {
    return 3.14 * c.radius * c.radius
}

// Square implements Shape
func (s Square) Area() float64 {
    return s.length * s.length
}

func calculateArea(listOfShapes []Shape) {
    for _, shape := range listOfShapes {
        fmt.Println("Area: ", shape.Area())
    }
}

func main() {
    c1 := Circle{radius: 5}
    s1 := Square{length: 6}

    shapes := []Shape{c1, s1}
    calculateArea(shapes)
}
```

Suppose you now have a new shape, Triangle, that you want to add to your program. In this case, you just need to define the struct for the Triangle shape and implement the Shape interface by providing the implementation for the Area() function:

```go
type Triangle struct {
    base    float64
    height float64
}

func (t Triangle) Area() float64 {
    return 0.5 * t.base * t.height
}
```

You can then add it to the array of shapes and calculate its area:

```
func main() {
    c1 := Circle{radius: 5}
    s1 := Square{length: 6}
    t1 := Triangle{base: 6, height: 8}

    shapes := []Shape{c1, s1, t1}
    calculateArea(shapes)
}
```

The preceding code snippet prints out the following output:

```
Area of shape is   78.53981633974483
Area of shape is   36
Area of shape is   24
```

Adding methods to a type that doesn't satisfy an interface

Although the Shape interface only has a single method signature, Area(), types that implement this interface are not restricted to only implementing the Area() method. They can implement additional method(s) if they need to.

Let's now also add an additional method named Circumference() to the Circle struct:

```
// Circle implements Shape
func (c Circle) Area() float64 {
    return math.Pi * math.Pow(c.radius, 2)
}

func (c Circle) Circumference() float64 {
    return 2 * math.Pi * c.radius
}
```

Apart from implementing the Shape interface, the Circle type now also has an additional method.

Using the Stringer interface

Interfaces may still seem abstract to you at this point, but you've actually been inadvertently exposed to interfaces (without your knowing it) if you've ever used the `Println()` function from the `fmt` package.

For example, suppose you have an array of two elements:

```
var s [2]string
s[0] = "Hello"
s[1] = "World"
```

When you print out the array using the `Println()` function:

```
fmt.Println(s)
```

You get the following output:

```
[Hello World]
```

And when you have a struct like this:

```
type Person struct {
    FirstName string
    LastName  string
    Age       int
}
```

Printing a variable of this type:

```
me := Person{"Wei-Meng", "Lee", 38}
fmt.Println(me)
```

yields the following output:

```
{Wei-Meng Lee 38}
```

So, how does the `fmt.Println()` function know how to format the output of the object or variable that it's trying to print? Turns out that the `fmt` package defines an interface called `Stringer`.

The `Stringer` interface is a type that describes itself as a string:

```
type Stringer interface {
    String() string
}
```

When you try to print some objects using the `fmt.Println()` function, the function looks at this interface to see how to print the value of the specified object. So, if you don't like the way the `Person` struct is printed out:

```
{Wei-Meng Lee 38}
```

You can always implement your own `Stringer` interface's `String()` function, like this:

```
type Person struct {
    FirstName string
    LastName  string
    Age       int
}

func (p Person) String() string {
    return fmt.Sprintf("%v %v (%d years old)",
        p.FirstName, p.LastName, p.Age)
}
```

TIP

Here you're overriding the default behavior for the struct's `String()` function.

Now when you print out the value of `me`:

```
me := Person{"Wei-Meng", "Lee", 38}
fmt.Println(me)
```

You see the following:

```
Wei-Meng Lee (38 years old)
```

Implementing multiple interfaces

A type can implement multiple interfaces. For our `Circle` struct in the earlier discussion, you can also implement the `Stringer` interface by implementing the `String()` method:

```
func (c Circle) String() string {
    return fmt.Sprintf(
        "Area is %v Circumference is %v",
        c.Area(), c.Circumference())
}
```

Now when you print out a variable of type `Circle` using the `fmt.Println()` function:

```
func main() {
    c1 := Circle{radius: 5, name: "c1"}
    fmt.Println(c1)
}
```

You see something like this:

```
Area is 78.53981633974483 Circumference is
31.41592653589793
```

Using an empty interface

In Go, an interface that has zero methods is called an empty interface. An empty interface is represented as follows:

```
interface{}
```

An empty interface has no methods, so all types actually implement the empty interface. An empty interface is useful when you want to handle data of unknown type. For example, you can have a function that accepts a parameter of type `interface{}`:

```
func doSomething(i interface{}) {
    fmt.Println(i)
}
```

When you call the function, you can pass in arguments of any type:

```
doSomething("Hi!")        // string
doSomething(3.14)         // float
doSomething([]int{3, 4})  // array
```

Determining whether a value implements a specific interface

Sometimes you want to check if a type implements a particular interface. For example, you want to check if a particular type implements the Shape interface. If it does, you can then call its Area() function. Using the example of the Circle type, assume that you have a variable of type Circle:

```
c1 := Circle{radius: 5, name: "c1"}
```

Next, assign c1 to an empty interface:

```
var v interface{} = c1
```

You can then use *type assertion* to gain access to an interface value's underlying concrete value. To check if c1 implements the Shape interface, assert it as Shape:

```
v, ok := v.(Shape)
```

TIP

Type assertion allows you to test if a value stored in an interface variable is of a particular type. For example, the following statement asserts that x is not nil and that the value stored in x is of type T:

```
x.(T)
```

The type assertion returns two values: the underlying value and a result indicating whether the assertion succeeded. If the assertion returns a true, it means the c1 implements the Shape interface, so you can call its Area() function:

```
if ok {
    fmt.Println(v.Area())
}
```

If the assertion returns a false, it means that either v is nil or it does not implement the Shape interface.

Multitasking
in Go

IN THIS PART . . .

Perform concurrent operations in Go using Goroutines.

See how Goroutines communicate using channels.

Chapter **11**

Threading Using Goroutines

I n the previous chapters, all the Go statements that I show you are executed sequentially: A statement will execute only after the previous statement has finished executing. However, in real life, we often do things concurrently — for example, you can be driving and at the same time listening to a podcast, a receptionist can answer the phone while greeting visitors in a busy reception area, and so on.

In programming, *concurrent programming* is a technique that allows you to perform multiple tasks at the same time. Concurrent programming often requires the use of constructs such as threads and locks to perform synchronization and prevent deadlocks. It's complex.

In Go, *goroutines* are functions that run concurrently with other functions. When you use goroutines, your program will be more responsive. You might use goroutines when performing tasks that deal with different input sources. For example, your program may need to interact with the users and at the same time need to communicate with backend servers through the network. Because network accesses typically incur significant network latency, it's common to run the function that accesses the network concurrently as a goroutine.

TIP

For readers who are already familiar with threading in other programming languages, think of goroutines as lightweight threads.

In this chapter, I explain the basics of goroutines and how you can synchronize them. You find out how goroutines work, how to safely share resources among goroutines, as well as how to synchronize goroutines.

Understanding Goroutines

The best way to understand goroutines is to use an example. Consider the following program:

```go
package main

import (
    "fmt"
    "time"
)

func say(s string, times int) {
    for i := 0; i < times; i++ {
        // inject a 100 ms delay
        time.Sleep(100 * time.Millisecond)
        fmt.Println(i, s)
    }
}

func main() {
    say("Hello", 3)
    say("World", 2)
}
```

In this program, you have a function named say(), which takes in two arguments: a string to print on the console and the number of times the string must be printed. In the main() function, you call the say() function two times: first with the string "Hello", and again with the string "World".

When you run the program, you see the following output:

```
0 Hello
1 Hello
2 Hello
0 World
1 World
```

This is what you expected because the first call to the say() function must end before the second call can proceed. But what if you want to make the two calls run concurrently? If you're a seasoned developer, you're familiar with a concept known as *threading*, which allows you to implement concurrent operations — multiple functions can all be running at the same time. To call the say() function concurrently in Go, you use goroutines.

In Go, a goroutine is a lightweight thread managed by the Go runtime. To run a function as a goroutine, simply call it using the go keyword:

```
func main() {
    go say("Hello", 3)
    go say("World", 2)
    fmt.Scanln()
}
```

The first statement calls the say() function as a goroutine. Essentially, it means "Run the say() function independently and immediately return control back to the calling statement." The second statement does the same. Now you have two separate instances of the say() function running concurrently. The result may appear like this (you may get a different result):

```
0 World
0 Hello
1 World
1 Hello
2 Hello
```

Each time you run this program, you may get a slightly different sequence of the words printed. This is because the Go runtime manages how this function runs, and you have no control over which is printed first. Notice that the main() function has the following statement:

```
fmt.Scanln()
```

Without this statement, you'd most likely be unable to see any outputs. This is because each time a goroutine is called, the control is immediately returned back to the calling statement. Without the Scanln() function to wait for user input, the program automatically terminates after the second goroutine is called. After the program is terminated, all goroutines are also terminated and no output will ever be printed.

TIP

If the main() function is terminated, all the goroutines currently running will also be terminated.

Using Goroutines with Shared Resources

Although goroutines makes it really easy for you to perform concurrent operations, you have to use them with care when your goroutines access shared resources (such as variables). For example, two Goroutines may concurrently access a single variable — one crediting some amount to it and another one debiting from it. It's important to ensure that when one Goroutine is adding values to the variable, another one is prevented from accessing it until the other Goroutine is done with it.

In the following sections, I explain the problems posed by multiple Goroutines trying to access the same shared resource, as well as the various techniques that you can use to resolve them.

Seeing how shared resources impact goroutines

Consider the following program where you have two functions:

>> The credit() function adds 100 to balance a total of five times.

>> The debit() function deducts 100 from balance a total of five times.

You called the credit() and debit() functions simultaneously as goroutines.

```go
package main

import (
    "fmt"
    "math/rand"
    "time"
)

var balance int

func credit() {
    for i := 0; i < 5; i++ {
        balance += 100
        time.Sleep(time.Duration(rand.Intn(100)) *
            time.Millisecond)
        fmt.Println("After crediting, balance is",
            balance)
    }
}
```

```go
func debit() {
    for i := 0; i < 5; i++ {
        balance -= 100
        time.Sleep(time.Duration(rand.Intn(100)) *
            time.Millisecond)
        fmt.Println("After debiting, balance is", balance)
    }
}

func main() {
    balance = 200
    fmt.Println("Initial balance is", balance)
    go credit()
    go debit()
    fmt.Scanln()
}
```

When you run the program, you may see something like the following:

```
Initial balance is 200
After crediting, balance is 200
After debiting, balance is 300
After crediting, balance is 200
After debiting, balance is 300
After debiting, balance is 200
After debiting, balance is 100
After crediting, balance is 0
After debiting, balance is 100
After crediting, balance is 100
After crediting, balance is 200
```

Notice anything wrong? The most obvious error is in the second line. If you look at the first line, the initial balance is 200. On the second line, it says that, after crediting, the balance is still 200? It should be 300. Why is it wrong?

After crediting the balance by 100 (where the balance should now be updated to 300), there was a delay of a random amount of time before the balance could be printed on the console. In the midst of this delay, the debit() function had a chance to deduct 100 from the balance (where the balance now would become 200). When the turn comes for the credit() function to continue printing the balance, it would now see 200 instead of 300. Figure 11-1 summarizes this flow of events.

Time

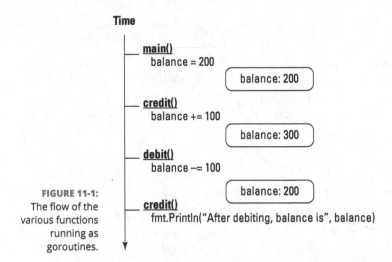

Although the final balance is 200, which is expected, this program is still not safe because the balance is not correctly printed during the process.

A more concerning situation might arise when the credit() function tries to increment the value of balance (which is initially 200) by 100. Before the incremented value (which should be 300) can be written to balance, the debit() function tries to decrement the balance (which it currently sees as 200) by 100. And before this decremented value can be written to balance, the credit() function now tries to write the value of 300 to balance. And finally, when the debit() function gets to execute it will now write the value of 100 to balance. The end result is that the balance variable is now in an inconsistent state (see Figure 11-2).

Time

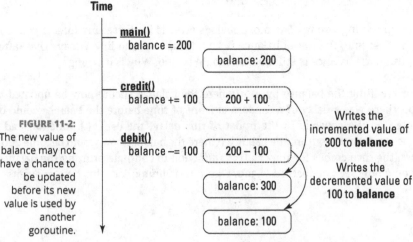

Accessing shared resources using mutual exclusion

As you can see from the previous section, when you have goroutines that access the same variable, it's important to make sure that only one goroutine can access the variable at any one time. To do so, you need to use the concept of *mutual exclusion* (also commonly known as *mutex*).

To implement mutual exclusion, Go's standard library provides the `Mutex` type (a struct) in the `sync` package. A `Mutex` is a *mutual exclusion lock.* A mutual exclusion lock is a technique to ensure exclusive access to shared data between threads of execution. When one Goroutine gains the mutual exclusion lock, other Goroutines need to wait until the lock is released.

The following program shows how you can use a `Mutex` object to enclose blocks of code to ensure that when one block is being executed by a goroutine, another block can't execute it:

```go
package main

import (
    "fmt"
    "math/rand"
    "sync"
    "time"
)

var balance int
var mutex = &sync.Mutex{}

func credit() {
    for i := 0; i < 5; i++ {
        mutex.Lock()
        balance += 100
        time.Sleep(time.Duration(rand.Intn(100)) * time.Millisecond)
        fmt.Println("After crediting, balance is", balance)
        mutex.Unlock()
    }
}

func debit() {
    for i := 0; i < 5; i++ {
        mutex.Lock()
        balance -= 100
        time.Sleep(time.Duration(rand.Intn(100)) * time.Millisecond)
```

```
        fmt.Println("After debiting, balance is", balance)
        mutex.Unlock()
    }
}

func main() {
    balance = 200
    fmt.Println("Initial balance is", balance)
    go credit()
    go debit()
    fmt.Scanln()
}
```

The Lock() and Unlock() functions of a Mutex object allows you to mark the start and end of a *critical section* (where not more than one goroutine can execute at the same time).

While one goroutine holds the lock, all other goroutines are prevented from executing any lines of code protected by the same mutex, and are forced to wait until the lock is unlocked before they can proceed.

The preceding program will now credit, debit, and print the balance variable correctly:

```
Initial balance is 200
After crediting, balance is 300
After crediting, balance is 400
After debiting, balance is 300
After crediting, balance is 400
After crediting, balance is 500
After debiting, balance is 400
After debiting, balance is 300
After crediting, balance is 400
After debiting, balance is 300
After debiting, balance is 200
```

Using atomic counters for modifying shared resources

In addition to using the Mutex object for marking critical sections, you can perform changes to shared variables in a thread-safe manner using *atomic counters* (routines that allow you to perform mathematical operations on variables one thread at a time). The atomic package provides low-level atomic memory primitives useful for implementing synchronization algorithms. So, instead of using the `Mutex` object to ensure that the `balance` variable is credited or debited correctly, use the `AddInt64()` function, like the following statements in bold:

```
package main

import (
    "fmt"
    "math/rand"
    "sync"
    "sync/atomic"
    "time"
)

var balance int64

func credit() {
    for i := 0; i < 10; i++ {
        // adds 100 to balance atomically
        atomic.AddInt64(&balance, 100)
        time.Sleep(time.Duration(rand.Intn(100)) * time.Millisecond)
    }
}

func debit() {
    for i := 0; i < 5; i++ {
        // deducts -100 from balance atomically
        atomic.AddInt64(&balance, -100)
        time.Sleep(time.Duration(rand.Intn(100)) * time.Millisecond)
    }
}

func main() {
    balance = 200
    fmt.Println("Initial balance is", balance)
    go credit()
    go debit()
    fmt.Scanln()
    fmt.Println(balance)
}
```

The `AddInt64()` function atomically adds a value to the specified variable (in which you pass the address of the variable to be modified using the & operator) and returns the new value. The `AddInt64()` function ensures that when one Goroutine is adding a value to the specified variable, no other Goroutine is allowed to modify the specified variable until the addition operation is done. It works just like the mutual exclusion lock example discussed in the previous section, without the need to call the Lock() and Unlock() functions of a Mutex object.

Note that the preceding code credits the balance variable ten times.

The preceding program prints out the following output:

```
Initial balance is 200
<Press enter after a while>
700
```

TIP

In this example, you only print out the balance after the two goroutines have finished crediting and debiting the values in the balance variable. If you want to print the balance in the credit() and debit() functions (as in the previous section), you have to use the Mutex object to ensure that immediately after crediting or debiting, the correct balance is printed.

Synchronizing Goroutines

When you have multiple Goroutines all running at the same time, you need to be able to synchronize them so that you have a way to coordinate the execution of your code. For example, you may have two Goroutines fetching data from different web services, and you need to ensure that these two Goroutines finish execution before you go ahead with the next block of code. In this scenario, there must be a way for you to know when the Goroutines are done.

If you check out the code snippets in the previous section, you see that there is a Scanln() function near the end of the main() function:

```
func main() {
    balance = 200
    fmt.Println("Initial balance is", balance)
    go credit()
    go debit()
    fmt.Scanln()
    fmt.Println(balance)
}
```

If you *don't* have the Scanln() function, the main() function will immediately exit after calling the two goroutines, and the balance printed will not be the correct final result.

The solution to this problem? Wait groups.

When you have multiple goroutines running and you want to know when they've completed, you can use a *wait group*. To use a wait group, you first create a variable of type sync.WaitGroup, like this:

```
var wg sync.WaitGroup
```

Now when you call a goroutine, simply call the wg.Add() function to add 1 to the WaitGroup counter:

```
wg.Add(1) // add 1 to the WaitGroup counter
```

When the goroutine that you've called has finished execution, call the wg.Done() function to decrement the WaitGroup counter by 1:

```
wg.Done() // decrement 1 from the WaitGroup counter
```

When you want to wait for the completion of all goroutines, use the wg.Wait() function:

```
wg.Wait() // blocks until WaitGroup counter is 0
```

The Wait() function blocks until the WaitGroup counter is 0. As soon as the Wait-Group counter reaches 0, this means that all goroutines have been completed and you can continue executing all ensuing statements.

Now that you understand how the WaitGroup works, let me show you how it can be applied to the earlier example:

```
package main

import (
    "fmt"
    "math/rand"
    "sync"
    "sync/atomic"
    "time"
)

var balance int64
```

```go
func credit(wg *sync.WaitGroup) {
    // notify the WaitGroup when we are done
    defer wg.Done()
    for i := 0; i < 10; i++ {
        // adds 100 to balance atomically
        atomic.AddInt64(&balance, 100)
        time.Sleep(time.Duration(rand.Intn(100)) * time.Millisecond)
    }

}

func debit(wg *sync.WaitGroup) {
    // notify the WaitGroup when we are done
    defer wg.Done()
    for i := 0; i < 5; i++ {
        // deducts -100 from balance atomically
        atomic.AddInt64(&balance, -100)
        time.Sleep(time.Duration(rand.Intn(100)) * time.Millisecond)
    }
}

func main() {
    var wg sync.WaitGroup

    balance = 200
    fmt.Println("Initial balance is", balance)

    wg.Add(1) // add 1 to the WaitGroup counter
    go credit(&wg)

    wg.Add(1) // add 1 to the WaitGroup counter
    go debit(&wg)

    wg.Wait() // blocks until WaitGroup counter is 0
    fmt.Println("Final balance is", balance)
}
```

In this example, I'm doing the following:

>> Creating a WaitGroup object

>> Calling the wg.Add() function to increment the WaitGroup counter prior to calling the credit() goroutine

>> Calling the wg.Add() function to increment the WaitGroup counter prior to calling the debit() goroutine

>> Calling the wg.Done() function in the credit() and debit() functions when I'm done either crediting or debiting the balance variable

>> Calling the wg.Wait() function to wait for the completion of the two goroutines

When the two goroutines are finally done, the WaitGroup counter becomes zero, and all statements blocked on wg.Wait() are released. The program will now print out the balance:

```
Initial balance is 200
Final balance is 700
```

If you want to print out the interim balance in the goroutines, you can use the Mutex object to mark out the critical section as you did earlier:

```
package main

import (
    "fmt"
    "math/rand"
    "sync"
    "sync/atomic"
    "time"
)

var balance int64
var mutex = &sync.Mutex{}

func credit(wg *sync.WaitGroup) {
    // notify the WaitGroup when we are done
    defer wg.Done()
    for i := 0; i < 10; i++ {
        mutex.Lock()
        // adds 100 to balance atomically
        atomic.AddInt64(&balance, 100)
        fmt.Println("After crediting, balance is", balance)
        mutex.Unlock()
        time.Sleep(time.Duration(rand.Intn(100)) * time.Millisecond)
    }
}

func debit(wg *sync.WaitGroup) {
    // notify the WaitGroup when we are done
    defer wg.Done()
```

```
    for i := 0; i < 5; i++ {
        mutex.Lock()
        // deducts -100 from balance atomically
        atomic.AddInt64(&balance, -100)
        fmt.Println("After debiting, balance is", balance)
        mutex.Unlock()
        time.Sleep(time.Duration(rand.Intn(100)) * time.Millisecond)
    }
}

func main() {
    var wg sync.WaitGroup
    balance = 200
    fmt.Println("Initial balance is", balance)

    wg.Add(1)
    go credit(&wg)

    wg.Add(1)
    go debit(&wg)

    wg.Wait()
    fmt.Println("Final balance is", balance)
}
```

Now you see the following output:

```
Initial balance is 200
After debiting, balance is 100
After crediting, balance is 200
After debiting, balance is 100
After crediting, balance is 200
After debiting, balance is 100
After crediting, balance is 200
After crediting, balance is 300
After crediting, balance is 400
After debiting, balance is 300
After crediting, balance is 400
After crediting, balance is 500
After debiting, balance is 400
After crediting, balance is 500
After crediting, balance is 600
After crediting, balance is 700
Final balance is 700
```

Chapter **12**

Communicating between Goroutines Using Channels

In Chapter 11, I introduce you to goroutines, one of the key features of the Go programming language. Goroutines are executed independently of one another and are a great way to implement concurrent programming. However, very often, goroutines need a way to communicate with each other in order to work properly. In Go, you can get goroutines to communicate with one another through pipes known as *channels.* In this chapter, I show you how channel works.

Understanding Channels

In Go, channels are the pipes that connect concurrent goroutines. You can send values into channels from one goroutine and receive those values in another goroutine. Think of channels as temporary storage for passing values between goroutines.

To create a channel, you use the make() function, together with the chan keyword and the type of data that you want the channel to store for you, like this:

```
ch := make(chan int)
```

To send a value into the channel, you use the <- operator. The following example writes the value 5 into the ch channel:

```
ch <- 5
```

To retrieve a value from the channel, simply put the channel variable to the right of the <- operator. The following example retrieves a value from the ch channel and assigns it to a variable named value:

```
value := <- ch
```

In the following sections, I give you an example of how channels work and show you some uses for channels.

How channels work

To understand how channels work, let's start off with a very simple example. Consider the following program, where you have two functions — sendData() and getData():

```
package main

import (
    "fmt"
    "time"
)

//---send data into a channel---
func sendData(ch chan string) {
    fmt.Println("Sending a string into channel...")
    time.Sleep(2 * time.Second)
    ch <- "Hello"
}

//---getting data from the channel---
func getData(ch chan string) {
    fmt.Println("String retrieved from channel:", <-ch)
}
func main() {
    ch := make(chan string)
```

```
    go sendData(ch)
    go getData(ch)

    fmt.Scanln()
}
```

In the `main()` function, you first create a channel using the `make()` function, `ch`, with the type of channel specified (`string`). This means that the channel can only contain values of type `string`. You then call the `sendData()` and `getData()` functions as goroutines. In the `sendData()` function, you first print out the sentence *Sending a string into channel...* After a delay of two seconds, you insert a string into the channel using the `<-` operator.

TIP

If the channel variable is to the left of the `<-` operator, you're *sending* a value into the channel. If the channel variable is to the right of the `<-` operator, you're *receiving* a value from the channel.

At the same time, when you run the `sendData()` function, you're also running the `getData()` function. Here, with `getData()`, you're trying to receive a value from the channel. Because there is currently no value in the channel (it won't have any value in it until two seconds later), the `getData()` function will block. The moment a value is available in the channel, the `getData()` function will unblock and retrieve the value from the channel. Hence, the output of the program will look like this:

```
Sending a string into channel...
[After a two-second delay]
String retrieved from channel: Hello
```

For this example, the type of channel you're creating is known as an *unbuffered channel.* In an unbuffered channel, the sender blocks until the value has been received by a receiver.

REMEMBER

When you try to retrieve a value from a channel and there is no value available, your code will block.

Let's now make the following changes to the program (shown in bold):

```
package main

import (
    "fmt"
    "time"
)
```

```
//---send data into a channel---
func sendData(ch chan string) {
    fmt.Println("Sending a string into channel...")
    // comment out the following line
    // time.Sleep(2 * time.Second)

    ch <- "Hello"
    fmt.Println("String has been retrieved from channel...")
}

//---getting data from the channel---
func getData(ch chan string) {
    time.Sleep(2 * time.Second)
    fmt.Println("String retrieved from channel:", <-ch)
}

func main() {
    ch := make(chan string)

    go sendData(ch)
    go getData(ch)

    fmt.Scanln()
}
```

Notice that in the sendData() function, you try to print a sentence immediately after sending a value into the channel. In the getData() function, you insert a two-second delay before you retrieve the value from the channel.

Let's run the program and see the output:

```
Sending a string into channel...
[After a two-second delay...]
String retrieved from channel: Hello
String has been retrieved from channel...
```

Notice that immediately after sending a value into the channel, the sendData() function is blocked. It will only resume after the value in the channel is retrieved by the getData() function.

When you send a value into an unbuffered channel, your code will block until the value is retrieved from the channel.

How channels are used

When you know how a channel works, you probably want to see some of the practical uses of channels and why you would want to use them in the first place.

Suppose you have a function named sum( ) that sums up a slice of integer values:

```go
func sum(s []int, c chan int) {
    sum := 0
    for _, v := range s {
        sum += v
    }
    c <- sum
}
```

The first argument to the sum( ) function is a slice of int values; the second argument is a channel of type int. When the numbers in the array have been summed up, the sum is written to the channel.

To use the sum( ) function, let's now generate ten random numbers and assign it to a variable named s:

```go
func main() {
    s := []int{}
    sliceSize := 10
    for i := 0; i < sliceSize; i++ {
        s = append(s, rand.Intn(100))
    }
}
```

If you try out this program, you'll realize that the random numbers are always the same. To get different random numbers every time you run the program, use the rand.Seed( ) function, which uses the provided seed value to initialize the generator to a deterministic state:

```go
rand.Seed(time.Now().UnixNano())
```

Although I only have ten items in this array, imagine if you had a million items. It would take some time to sum up all the numbers in the slide. So, it would be a good idea to split the numbers into smaller groups and use goroutines to sum them up concurrently.

In this example, I'll split this slice into five parts, take each part and pass it to the sum() function together with the channel c, and call it as a goroutine:

```
func main() {
    s := []int{}
    sliceSize := 10
    for i := 0; i < sliceSize; i++ {
        s = append(s, rand.Intn(100))
    }

    c := make(chan int)
    partSize := 2
    parts := sliceSize / partSize
    i := 0
    for i < parts {
        go sum(s[i*partSize:(i+1)*partSize], c)
        i += 1
    }
}
```

Essentially, I'm breaking up the array into five parts and trying to sum each part concurrently. As each goroutine finishes the summing process, it writes the partial sum to the channel, as shown in Figure 12-1.

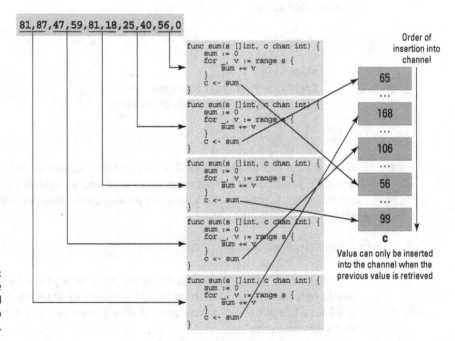

FIGURE 12-1:
Each goroutine tries to send the partial sum to the channel.

Channels behave like queues: All items are retrieved in the same order that they were written (first in, first out). As each goroutine writes to the channel, it's blocked until its values in the channels are received.

REMEMBER

After the first goroutine has sent a value into the channel, it's blocked until the value is retrieved from the channel. Meanwhile, the other four goroutines trying to also send in values to the channel will be blocked until the value is removed from the channel. They get the chance to send a value into the channel on a first-come, first-served basis.

Because you know that you have five separate goroutines (and, therefore, a total of five values to be written to the channel), you can write a loop and try to extract the values in the channel:

```go
func main() {
    s := []int{}
    sliceSize := 10
    for i := 0; i < sliceSize; i++ {
        s = append(s, rand.Intn(100))
    }

    c := make(chan int)
    partSize := 2
    parts := sliceSize / partSize
    i := 0
    for i < parts {
        go sum(s[i*partSize:(i+1)*partSize], c)
        i += 1
    }

    i = 0
    total := 0
    for i < parts {
        partialSum := <-c          // read from channel
        fmt.Println("Partial Sum: ", partialSum)
        total += partialSum
        i += 1
    }
    fmt.Println("Total: ", total)
    fmt.Scanln()
}
```

Each value in the channel represents the partial sum of the values in each array. It's important to remember that when you send a value into an unbuffered channel, the goroutine is blocked until the value is received by another function/

goroutine. Likewise, when you're reading a value from a channel, your code is blocked until the data is read from the channel. If the goroutines are taking a long time to sum up, the preceding code snippet will block until all the partial sums are retrieved.

Iterating through Channels

In the previous section, I knew that there were five goroutines trying to calculate the sum of a series of numbers and that each result was going to be sent to the channel. So, I tried to read from the channel five times and sum up the partial totals. However, in some situations, you may not know in advance how many values there may be in the channel. This is where the range keyword comes in handy.

Consider the following example:

```go
package main

import (
    "fmt"
    "time"
)

func fib(n int, c chan int) {
    a, b := 1, 1
    for i := 0; i < n; i++ {
        c <- a              // blocked until value is received from channel
        a, b = b, a + b
        time.Sleep(1 * time.Second)
    }
    close(c)                // close the channel
}

func main() {
    c := make(chan int)
    go fib(10, c)
    for i := range c {   // read from channel until channel is closed
        fmt.Println(i)
    }
}
```

In this example, you have a function named fib() that takes in two arguments — the number of elements to generate for the Fibonacci sequence, and the channel to store the numbers in. Each number of the Fibonacci sequence is calculated and then sent into the channel. I've added a delay of one second for each number to simulate some delay. As each Fibonacci number is being generated and inserted into the channel, the fib() function blocks until the value is retrieved from the channel. After generating all the required Fibonacci numbers, you close the channel (using the close() function) to indicate that the channel is no longer accepting values.

REMEMBER

For an unbuffered channel, after a value is sent to the channel, the sender blocks until the value is retrieved from the channel.

In the main() function, you first create an instance of the channel using the make() function, and then proceed to call the fib() function as a goroutine — generating the first ten Fibonacci numbers.

You use the range keyword on the c channel to keep on reading values until the channel is closed. You should now see the following output:

```
1
1
2
3
5
8
13
21
34
55
```

It's important to note that the range keyword will continuously read values from a channel repeatedly until the channel is closed. Failure to close the channel will cause a fatal error: all goroutines are asleep - deadlock! error.

Asynchronously Waiting on Channels

In the real world, you may have a few goroutines running and simultaneously sending values into different channels. Consider the following example:

```
package main

import (
    "fmt"
    "time"
)
```

```go
func fib(n int, c chan int) {
    a, b := 1, 1
    for i := 0; i < n; i++ {
        c <- a
        a, b = b, a+b
        time.Sleep(2 * time.Second)
    }
    close(c)
}

func counter(n int, c chan int) {
    for i := 0; i < n; i++ {
        c <- i
        time.Sleep(1 * time.Second)
    }
    close(c)
}

func main() {
    c1 := make(chan int)
    c2 := make(chan int)

    go fib(10, c1)          // generate 10 fibo nums
    go counter(10, c2)      // generate 10 numbers

    for i := range c1 {
        fmt.Println("fib()", i)
    }

    for i := range c2 {
        fmt.Println("counter()", i)
    }
}
```

In this example, you call the fib() and counter() functions as goroutines. These two goroutines independently write values into two different channels: c1 and c2. As usual, I've inserted delay statements in both functions to simulate different speeds in which the values are written into the channels. When the functions are done, the channels are closed.

Next, you range the channels to print out the values in the two channels. You should see the following:

```
fib() 1
fib() 1
fib() 2
fib() 3
fib() 5
fib() 8
fib() 13
fib() 21
fib() 34
fib() 55
counter() 0
counter() 1
counter() 2
counter() 3
counter() 4
counter() 5
counter() 6
counter() 7
counter() 8
counter() 9
```

But there is one problem here. Notice that all the numbers generated by the fib()
function are printed before those generated by the counter() function are printed.
This is because the first for loop needs to complete before the second for loop can
commence.

Ideally, the numbers should be printed whenever they're available. Moreover, the
numbers generated by the counter() function should be printed earlier because
the delay is shorter than it is with the fib() function.

To solve this problem, you can use a for loop, together with the select statement, like the following statements in bold:

```
func main() {
    c1 := make(chan int)
    c2 := make(chan int)

    go fib(10, c1)        // generate 10 Fibonacci numbers
    go counter(10, c2)    // generate 10 numbers

    c1Closed := false
    c2Closed := false

    for {
        select {
```

```
        case n, ok := <-c1:
            if !ok {
                // channel closed and drained
                c1Closed = true
                if c1Closed && c2Closed {
                    return
                }
            } else {
                fmt.Println("fib()", n)
            }
        case m, ok := <c2:
            if !ok {
                // channel closed and drained
                c2Closed = true
                if c1Closed && c2Closed {
                    return
                }
            } else {
                fmt.Println("counter()", m)
            }
        }
    }
}
```

In each `case` block, you retrieve a value from the respective channel. Note that in this example, you retrieve the value from the channel and assign it to a pair of variables:

```
n, ok := <-c1
```

The first variable contains the value retrieved from the channel, while the second variable contains a Boolean value to indicate if the retrieving is successful. If the value is `false`, this indicates that the channel is already closed. The preceding statements will retrieve the values from both channels until both channels are closed. You should now see the following results:

```
fib() 1
counter() 0
counter() 1
fib() 1
counter() 2
counter() 3
fib() 2
counter() 4
```

```
counter() 5
fib() 3
counter() 6
counter() 7
fib() 5
counter() 8
counter() 9
fib() 8
fib() 13
fib() 21
fib() 34
fib() 55
```

Note that when both channels are closed, the main function will exit, as indicated by the `return` statement. If you want to perform some other functions in the `main()` function while at the same time retrieving the values from the two channels, run the `for` loop as a goroutine:

```go
func main() {
    c1 := make(chan int)
    c2 := make(chan int)

    go fib(10, c1)
    go counter(10, c2)

    c1Closed := false
    c2Closed := false

    go func() {
        for {
            select {
            case n, ok := <-c1:
                ...

            case m, ok := <-c2:
                ...

            }
        }
    }()

    fmt.Println("Continue to do something else...")
    fmt.Scanln() // needed here to prevent the program from existing before all
                 // the channel values are read
}
```

Using Buffered Channels

So far, all my discussion on channels has centered on *unbuffered channels*. When you send a value to an unbuffered channel, your code will block until the value is received from the channel. Likewise, when you read from an unbuffered channel, your code will block until a value is available and retrieved from the channel.

A *buffered channel*, on the other hand, allows multiple values to be stored in the channel. Your code will only block when you try to send a value to a channel that is full or when you try to read from an empty channel.

To create a buffered channel, provide the buffer length as the second argument to the make() function when you initialize a channel:

```
c := make(chan int, 10)
```

This statement creates a buffered channel with buffer size 10. In other words, the channel can contain up to ten values before the sending code will block. An unbuffered channel is equivalent to a buffered channel of length 0:

```
c := make(chan int, 0)  // unbuffered channel
```

So, when do you use a buffered channel? Buffered channels are useful if the send rate is higher than the retrieval rate. Or when you want the sender to continue execution after a value has been sent to the channel without waiting for the value to be retrieved.

Using the example from earlier, where you compute the sum of a slice of numbers, you can now create a buffered channel of length 5:

```
func sum(s []int, c chan int) {
    sum := 0
    for _, v := range s {
        sum += v
    }
    c <- sum
    fmt.Println("Done and can continue to do other work")
}

func main() {
    s := []int{}
    sliceSize := 10
```

```go
    for i := 0; i < sliceSize; i++ {
        s = append(s, rand.Intn(100))
    }

    c := make(chan int, 5) // buffered channel of length 5
    partSize := 2
    parts := sliceSize / partSize
    i := 0
    for i < parts {
        go sum(s[i*partSize:(i+1)*partSize], c)
        i += 1
    }

    i = 0
    total := 0
    time.Sleep(1 * time.Second) // simulate retrieving at a later time
    for i < parts {
        partialSum := <-c // read from channel
        fmt.Println("Partial Sum: ", partialSum)
        total += partialSum
        i += 1
    }
    fmt.Println("Total: ", total)
    fmt.Scanln()
}
```

When you run the program, you'll now see that after summing up the partial slice of numbers, the sum() function won't be blocked and can continue to execute other tasks:

```
Done and can continue to do other work
Done and can continue to do other work
Done and can continue to do other work
Done and can continue to do other work
Done and can continue to do other work
Partial Sum:   168
Partial Sum:   99
Partial Sum:   56
Partial Sum:   106
Partial Sum:   65
Total:   494
```

As an exercise, try to reduce the length of the channel and notice the output.

4

Organizing Your Code

Chapter **13**

Using and Creating Packages in Go

G o uses the concept of *packages* to better organize code for reusability and readability. In earlier chapters, I show you how to use some of the built-in packages like `fmt`, `strconv`, `math`, and `time` in your Go application. In this chapter, I dig into the topic of packages in more detail. I show you how to create your own packages for your own use, as well as create packages for sharing. Finally, I explain how to install third-party packages on your system.

Working with Packages

If you've read the earlier chapters in this book, you know that Go applications always have this first statement:

```
package main
```

Go organizes code into units call *packages*. A package is made up of a collection of files. The `main` package is a special package that contains the `main()` function, which makes the main package an executable program. The `main()` function serves as the entry point to your application.

All files in a package must be in the same directory, and all package names must all be in lowercase.

Let's take a look at an example. Suppose you have a directory named my_app in your home directory, and in that directory is a file named main.go:

```
$HOME
 |__my_app
    |__main.go
```

The content of the main.go file looks like this:

```
package main

import (
    "fmt"
    "math"
)

type Point struct {
    X float64
    Y float64
}

func (p Point) length() float64 {
    return math.Sqrt(math.Pow(p.X, 2.0) + math.Pow(p.Y, 2.0))
}

func main() {
    pt1 := Point{X: 2, Y: 3}
    fmt.Println(pt1)
    fmt.Println(pt1.length())
}
```

TIP

The file that contains the main() function is usually named main.go, but this naming convention isn't mandatory — you can use any name you like.

Notice that the package is named main, so it has the main() function. You can extract the definition of the Point struct, as well as its method length() to another file (say, point.go), and put it in the same directory as main.go:

```
$HOME
 |__my_app
    |__main.go
    |__point.go
```

The `point.go` file now looks like this:

```go
package main

import (
    "math"
)

type Point struct {
    X float64
    Y float64
}

func (p Point) length() float64 {
    return math.Sqrt(math.Pow(p.X, 2.0) + math.Pow(p.Y, 2.0))
}
```

TIP

It's always useful to logically separate your code into as many files as needed. This will make maintenance of your code easier.

Make sure that the first line still uses the same `main` package name. With the `Point` struct and the `length()` method removed, `main.go` now looks like this:

```go
package main

import (
    "fmt"
)

func main() {
    pt1 := Point{X: 2, Y: 3}
    fmt.Println(pt1)
    fmt.Println(pt1.length())
}
```

Because these two files — `main.go` and `point.go` — both reside in the same directory and have the same package name (`main`), they belong to the same package. To run the preceding application, type the following commands in Terminal or Command Prompt:

```
$ cd ~/my_app
$ go run *.go
{2 3}
3.605551275463989
```

TIP

Note that you use `go run *.go` instead of `go run main.go`. You're now telling the Go compiler to search all the Go files for the main package with the `main()` function (because you've now divided the package into multiple physical files). Note that for Windows users, you need to use `go run`.

Figure 13-1 shows the `main` package with two physical files.

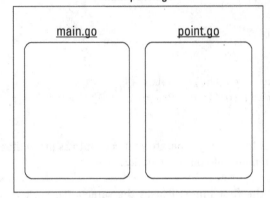

main package

main.go

point.go

FIGURE 13-1:
The main package is made up of two physical files.

For the preceding example to work, you need to ensure:

» Both files are in the same directory.

» Both packages have the same package name (`main`).

» One of the files has a `main()` function.

In the following sections, I show you how to create shareable packages and how to organize them into folders.

Creating shareable packages

In the previous section, I explain that your `main` package can be split into two physical files: `main.go` and `point.go`. The aim of putting the code for the `Point` struct and the `Length()` functions into a separate file is to allow you to separate and reuse the code. However, you can only reuse this code in the `main` package.

Imagine you're writing another program, and you also need to use the functions inside the `point.go` file. One way to do this would be to copy the `point.go` file into the same folder as your new project. The problem is, this approach isn't efficient. Plus, eventually, you may want to upgrade or bug-fix the `point.go` file, and if each project has a separate copy of point.go, this will make updating a nightmare.

A better idea would be to install point.go as a separate package that can be used by other apps, just as the fmt package that you use for console operations (such as printing) can be used by other apps.

To create a shareable package, first use the go env command to find out the location of the GOPATH environment variable:

```
$ go env
GO111MODULE=""
GOARCH="amd64"
...
GONOSUMDB=""
GOOS="darwin"
GOPATH="/Users/weimenglee/go"
GOPRIVATE=""
...
```

In this example, the GOPATH is pointing to the go folder in my home directory (/Users/weimenglee). Windows users should see their default GOPATH folder to be C:\Users\<username>\go.

So, let's now create a folder named src (if it doesn't already exist). Within the src folder, create another directory called geometry. Put the point.go file in the geometry folder:

```
$GOPATH (which is /Users/weimenglee/go)
  |__src
    |__geometry
      |__point.go
```

Modify the package name in point.go to geometry:

```
package geometry

import (
    "math"
)

type Point struct {
    X float64
    Y float64
}
```

```
func (p Point) Length() float64 {
    return math.Sqrt(math.Pow(p.X, 2.0) + math.Pow(p.Y, 2.0))
}
```

TIP

Note that in this example, the first letter of the Length() function is capitalized. In Go, any function name that starts with a capital letter can be accessed outside the package, while any function name that does not start with a capital letter can only be accessed internally, within the package. If the function is named length(), it won't be visible to other packages.

To install the package on the local computer, you need to change the directory to the geometry directory and use the go install command, like this:

```
$ cd ~/go/src/geometry
$ go install
```

In the original main.go file, to use the Point struct you now need to import the geometry package and, at the same time, prefix the Point struct with the geometry package name, like this:

```
package main

import (
    "fmt"
    "geometry"
)

func main() {
    pt1 := geometry.Point{X: 2, Y: 3}
    fmt.Println(pt1)
    fmt.Println(pt1.Length())
}
```

To run the program, simply use the go run command:

```
$ go run main.go
{2 3}
3.605551275463989
```

Organizing packages using directories

In the preceding section, you created a package named geometry. But let's assume that you want to create different packages related to geometry. There are several types of geometry (coordinate geometry, Euclidean geometry, analytic geometry, and so on).

Let's say the package you've created is related more to coordinate geometry, so it would be a good idea to create a subdirectory under the geometry directory, and then place the point.go under this new subdirectory, like this:

```
$GOPATH
  |__src
    |__geometry
      |__coordinate
        |__point.go
```

The point.go should now change its package name to coordinate:

```go
// Package coordinate for coordinate geometry
package coordinate

import (
    "math"
)

// Point represents a point in the 2-D coordinate space
type Point struct {
    X float64
    Y float64
}

// Length calculates the length of point from the origin
func (p Point) Length() float64 {
    return math.Sqrt(math.Pow(p.X, 2.0) + math.Pow(p.Y, 2.0))
}
```

To install the package on the local computer, you need to change the directory to the coordinate directory and use the go install command, like the following:

```
$ cd ~/go/src/geometry/coordinate
$ go install
```

TIP

The preceding ~/go directory refers to the folder pointed to by your GOPATH environment variable.

In the original `main.go` file, in order to use the `Point` struct, you now need to import the `geometry/coordinate` package. To use the `Point` struct, prefix it with the last path of the package name, which is `coordinate`:

```go
package main

import (
    "fmt"
    "geometry/coordinate"
)

func main() {
    pt1 := coordinate.Point{X: 2, Y: 3}
    fmt.Println(pt1)
    fmt.Println(pt1.Length())
}
```

Using Third-Party Packages

Go ships with a set of standard libraries for you to use in your program. These libraries are adequate to address most of your basic programming needs. But eventually, you'll probably want to do more. Fortunately, Go has a very vibrant developer community that creates and shares lots of useful third-party libraries.

Unlike languages like Python and JavaScript, where you can download third-party packages from central repositories like PyPI (https://pypi.org) or npm (www.npmjs.com), Go doesn't have a centralized official package registry. Instead, you fetch third-party packages through a hostname and path (think of GitHub).

To download and install packages, you use the `go get` command. The `get` command downloads the package named by the import paths, along with their dependencies. In the following sections, you see two examples of installing third-party packages: Emojis for Go and the Go Documentation package.

Emojis for Go

Want to add a little fun to your Go program? How about displaying some emojis? For this, you can use a Go package located at https://github.com/hackebrot/turtle that allows you to obtain emojis based on names. To install this package, you simply use the `go get` command followed by the URL of the package (without the https://), like this:

```
$ go get github.com/hackebrot/turtle
```

When you do that, the github.com/hackebrot/turtle package will be installed in the $GOPATH/src folder of your local computer, like this:

```
$GOPATH
  |__src
  |  |__github.com
  |  |   |__hackebrot
  |  |   |   |__turtle
  |  |   |   |   |__ ...
  |  |   |   |   |__ ...
```

To use this package, you simply import it into your package, like this:

```go
package main

import (
    "fmt"
    "github.com/hackebrot/turtle"
)

func main() {
    emoji, ok := turtle.Emojis["smiley"]
    if !ok {
        fmt.Println("No emoji found.")
    } else {
        fmt.Println(emoji.Char)
    }
}
```

The output for the preceding program shows a smiley face (☺).

Go Documentation

Go Documentation (Godoc for short) is a documentation generator for Go programs. By default, Godoc looks at the packages installed on your computer by examining the values in the $GOROOT and $GOPATH environment variables. It then runs a web server and presents the documentation it generated as web pages.

The steps for installing godoc depend on the operating system you're using:

Windows

On Windows, you can install godoc by using the go get command:

```
C:\Users\Wei-Meng Lee>go get golang.org/x/tools/cmd/godoc
```

After godoc is downloaded and installed, you can start the web server by specifying the following command:

```
C:\Users\Wei-Meng Lee>godoc -http=:6060
```

This command starts the godoc as a web server listening at port 6060. You can now use this URL (http://localhost:6060) to view the documentation of your Go packages on your computer (see Figure 13-2).

macOS

On the Mac, download and install godoc:

```
$ go get golang.org/x/tools/cmd/godoc
```

Next, create a file named org.golang.godoc.plist and then save it in the ~/Library/LaunchAgents/ directory. Populate the org.golang.godoc.plist file as follows:

```
<plist version="1.0">
<dict>
  <key>Label</key>
  <string>org.golang.godoc</string>
  <key>ProgramArguments</key>
  <array>
    <string>/Users/weimenglee/go/bin/godoc</string>
    <string>-http=localhost:6060</string>
  </array>
  <key>KeepAlive</key>
  <true/>
  <key>RunAtLoad</key>
  <true/>
  <key>WorkingDirectory</key>
  <string>/tmp</string>
</dict>
</plist>
```

The /Users/weimenglee/go/bin/godoc bit above represents the path to the godoc package on my computer. Change it to your own path. In particular, change /Users/weimenglee/go/ to your directory as specified in the GOPATH environment variable.

To run the godoc as a web server, type the following command in Terminal:

```
$ launchctl load ~/Library/LaunchAgents/org.golang.godoc.plist
```

This command starts the godoc as a web server listening at port 6060. You can now use this URL (http://localhost:6060) to view the documentation of your Go packages on your computer (see Figure 13-2).

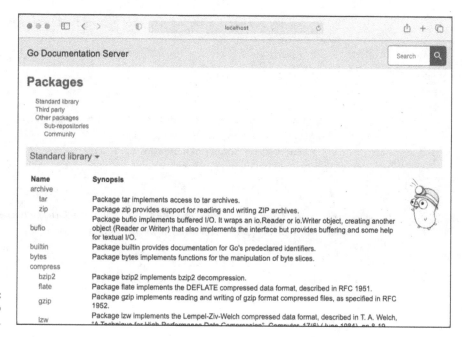

FIGURE 13-2:
The godoc web
pages.

To stop the godoc web server, use the following command:

```
$ launchctl unload ~/Library/LaunchAgents/org.golang.godoc.plist
```

FINDING THE DOCUMENTATION FOR THE COORDINATE PACKAGE

Here's something cool about the godoc package. Remember the point.go file in the earlier example? Did you notice the comments within the file?

```go
// Package coordinate for coordinate geometry
package coordinate

import (
    "math"
)

// Point represents a point in the 2-D coordinate space
type Point struct {
    X float64
    Y float64
}

// Length calculates the length of point from the origin
func (p Point) Length() float64 {
    return math.Sqrt(math.Pow(p.X, 2.0) +
        math.Pow(p.Y, 2.0))
}
```

If you now go to the godoc page, you'll be able to find the geometry package (listed under Third party; see the following figure).

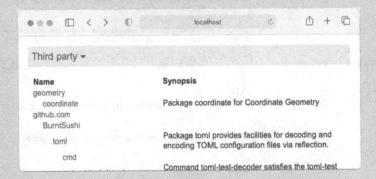

Clicking the geometry name will show you the packages and their descriptions contained within it (see the following figure).

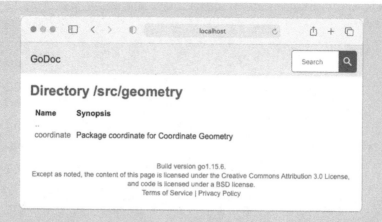

Clicking the `coordinate` package name will show the content and documentation of the package (see the following figure).

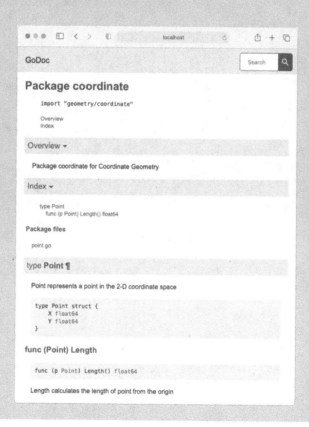

Chapter **14**

Grouping Packages into Modules

I n Go, a *module* is a directory of packages, with a file named go.mod at its root. The go.mod file defines the module's path, as well as the dependency requirements (that is, the packages and modules that are needed by this module in order for it to work correctly).

The best way to understand what is a module is to actually create one. In this chapter, I explain how to convert a group of packages into a module so that you can publish it and make it available for use by other Go developers.

Creating a Module

When you create a module, you can publish it and make it available for use by other Go developers. To create a module, follow these steps:

1. Create the following directories on your computer:

```
$HOME
    |__stringmod
      |__strings
      |__quotes
```

This code creates a module named stringmod, with a subdirectory named strings. The idea is to group related functionalities into directories so as to logically group them together. The strings folder should contain functions related to strings. In this example, stringmod is a module and strings and quotes are packages.

Now you're ready to add packages to the module.

2. **Add a file named** strings.go **to the** strings **directory and a file named** quotes.go **to the** quotes **directory.**

It should look like this:

```
$HOME
  |__stringmod
     |__strings
        |__strings.go
     |__quotes
        |__quotes.go
```

3. **Populate the** strings.go **file with the following statements:**

```
package strings

func internalFunction() {
    // In Go, a name is exported (visible outside the package) if it
    begins
    // with a capital letter
}

// Must begin with a capital letter in order to be exported
func CountOddEven(s string) (odds, evens int) {
    odds, evens = 0, 0
    for _, c := range s {
        if int(c)%2 == 0 {
            evens++
        } else {
            odds++
        }
    }
    return
}
```

4. Populate the quotes.go file with the following statements:

```
package quotes

import (
    "github.com/hackebrot/turtle"
)

func GetEmoji(name string) string {
    emoji, ok := turtle.Emojis[name]
    if !ok {
        return ""
    }
    return emoji.Char
}
```

TIP

Notice that the quotes package has a *dependency* on an external package, github.com/hackebrot/turtle.

Now you're ready to create the go.mod file.

5. In Terminal or Command Prompt, type the following commands:

```
$ cd ~/stringmod
$ go mod init github.com/weimenglee/stringmod
go: creating new go.mod: module
github.com/weimenglee/stringmod
```

TIP

For this example, I'm making my module available for download on GitHub. I've set the download URL as github.com/weimenglee/stringmod. For your own example, you should change the URL to your own repository URL (if you're using GitHub).

The go mod init command creates a go.mod file in the stringmod directory:

```
$HOME
  |__stringmod
    |__go.mod
    |__strings
      |__strings.go
    |__quotes
      |__quotes.go
```

The content of go.mod is:

```
module github.com/weimenglee/stringmod

go 1.15
```

The role of the go.mod file is to define the module's path so it can be imported and used by other packages.

Testing and Building a Module

After you've created a module, you're ready to test it. You can do that by trying to import it into another package and using it. Follow these steps:

1. **Add a new file named** main.go **in the** stringmod **folder:**

```
$HOME
   |__stringmod
      |__go.mod
      |__main.go
      |__strings
         |__strings.go
      |__quotes
         |__quotes.go
```

2. **Populate the** main.go **file as follows:**

```
package main

import (
    "fmt"

    "github.com/weimenglee/stringmod/quotes"
    "github.com/weimenglee/stringmod/strings"
)

func main() {
    o, e := strings.CountOddEven("12345")
    fmt.Println(o, e) // 3 2

    fmt.Println(quotes.GetEmoji("turtle"))
}
```

TIP

Notice that you're importing the two packages inside the `stringmod` modules using the `github.com/weimenglee/stringmod` import path:

```
"github.com/weimenglee/stringmod/strings"
"github.com/weimenglee/stringmod/quotes"
```

TIP

Also notice that the packages are referred to using their last names in the package path `github.com/weimenglee/stringmod/strings` and `github.com/weimenglee/stringmod/quotes`. If you don't want to use the last name in the package path, you can also provide aliases for the packages during import, like this:

```
package main

import (
  "fmt"
  str "github.com/weimenglee/stringmod/strings"
  qt "github.com/weimenglee/stringmod/quotes"
)

func main() {
    o, e := str.CountOddEven("12345")
    fmt.Println(o,e) // 3 2

    fmt.Println(qt.GetEmoji("turtle"))
}
```

You can now build the module. Type the following command in Terminal or Command Prompt to build the module:

```
$ cd ~/stringmod
$ go build
go: finding github.com/hackebrot/turtle v0.1.0
go: downloading github.com/hackebrot/turtle v0.1.0
```

During the build process, the package (`github.com/hackebrot/turtle`) required by the `quotes` package is downloaded and installed on your local computer at `$GOPATH/pkg/mod/`:

```
$GOPATH
  |__pkg
    |__mod
      |__github.com
        |__hackebrot
```

```
|__turtle@v0.1.0
  |__ ...
  |__ ...
```

REMEMBER

The default $GOPATH on my computer is /Users/weimenglee/go.

The content of the go.mod file now becomes the following:

```
module github.com/weimenglee/stringmod

go 1.15

require github.com/hackebrot/turtle v0.1.0
```

The go.mod file lists all the dependencies required by the packages inside the module.

One additional file is created: go.sum. This file contains the expected cryptographic checksums of the content of specific module versions. It looks like this:

```
github.com/hackebrot/turtle v0.1.0
  h1:cmS72nZuooIARtgix6IRPvmw8r4u8o1EZW02Q3DB8YQ=
github.com/hackebrot/turtle v0.1.0/go.mod
  h1:vDjX4rgnTSlvROhwGbE2GiB43F/1/8V5TXoRJL2cYTs=
```

You can now test the program to see if it runs correctly:

```
$ cd ~/stringmod
$ go run main.go
```

You should now see the following output:

```
3 2
[Emoji of a turtle]
```

Publishing a Module on GitHub

So far, you've created and tested your module running locally on your computer. To share it with the world, though, you need to publish it to an online repository, such as GitHub. In this section, I'm going to publish the module to GitHub, accessible through the following link: https://github.com/weimenglee/stringmod.

TIP

To publish to GitHub, the first thing you need is a GitHub account. Head over to `https://github.com/` and sign up for an account if you don't already have one.

After you've created a GitHub account, follow these steps:

1. **Sign in to your account.**

2. **In the Repositories section, click the New button (see Figure 14-1).**

FIGURE 14-1: Creating a new repository on GitHub.

3. **Name the repository stringmod and click the Create Repository button at the bottom of the page (see Figure 14-2).**

   After the repository is created, you need to upload the source code of your module.

4. **Click the Uploading an Existing File link (see Figure 14-3).**

   You should now see the page shown in Figure 14-4.

5. **Drag and drop the files and folders contained within the** `stringmod` **folder onto the rectangle on the GitHub page (see Figure 14-5).**

6. **After all the files and folders are uploaded, click the Commit Changes button at the bottom of the page (see Figure 14-6).**

   Your module is now published on GitHub (see Figure 14-7).

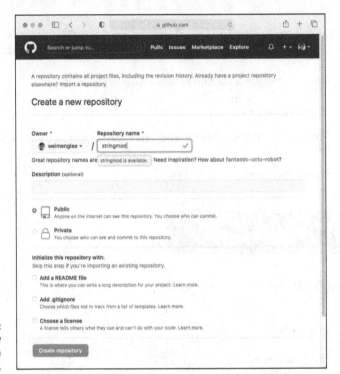

FIGURE 14-2:
Naming your new repository on GitHub.

FIGURE 14-3:
Getting ready to upload your files to GitHub.

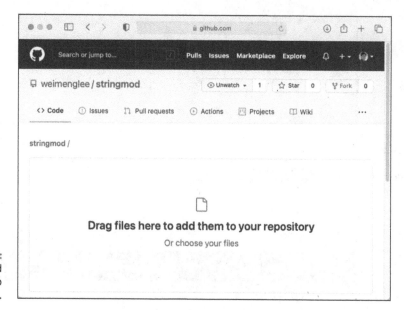

FIGURE 14-4:
You can drag and
drop the files to
GitHub.

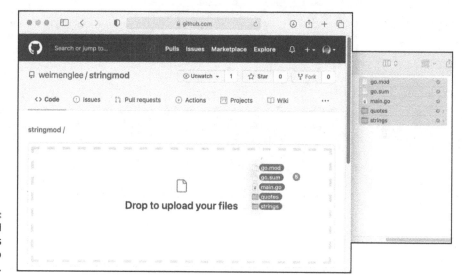

FIGURE 14-5:
Dragging and
dropping files
and folders to
GitHub.

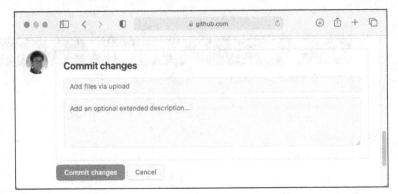

FIGURE 14-6:
Click the Commit
Changes button
to upload the files
and folders to
GitHub.

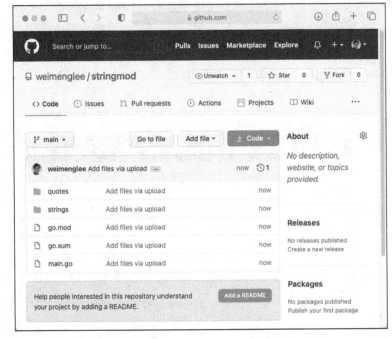

FIGURE 14-7:
The module is
now published!

To install this newly published module on your local computer, use the following
command:

```
$ go get github.com/weimenglee/stringmod
```

Remember to change the path to reflect your own package.

The package will be downloaded and installed in the $GOPATH/src/ and $GOPATH/bin/ folders:

```
$GOPATH
  |__src
  |  |__github.com
  |  |  |__hackebrot
  |  |  |  |__turtle
  |  |  |  |  |__ ...
  |  |  |  |  |__ ...
  |  |  |__weimenglee
  |  |     |__stringmod
  |  |     |__main.go
  |  |     |__quotes
  |  |        |__quotes.go
  |  |     |__strings
  |  |        |__strings.go
  |__bin
     |__stringmod
```

TIP

The dependencies of the `stringmod` module (which is the `github.com/hackebrot/turtle` module) will also be downloaded.

Because the `stringmod` module contains a `main` package (`main.go`) in the root directory, an executable file named `stringmod` will also be created in the $GOPATH/bin directory.

To use the module in your own package, you can import it into your application just as you did earlier:

```
package main

import (
    "fmt"

    "github.com/weimenglee/stringmod/quotes"
    "github.com/weimenglee/stringmod/strings"
)

func main() {
    ...
}
```

TIP

Go uses a number of directories to store modules and packages. Table 14-1 shows the various subdirectories in your $GOPATH directory and their uses. To find out the value of your GOPATH, use the go env command.

TABLE 14-1   Subdirectories within $GOPATH

Subdirectories in $GOPATH	Description
src	Contains the source code of packages that you've created or installed on your computer (modules that you've installed through the go get command).
bin	Contains the binary executables of Go modules that have the main package (and therefore contains the main() function) in the root directory. If you installed a module that does not contain the main package, it will have no entry in this directory.
pkg	Contains the non-executable packages. These packages are typically imported by other applications or modules.

5
Seeing Go in Action

Chapter **15**

Consuming Web APIs Using Go

When you have a good foundation in the Go programming language, it's time to put things into action! And you do that with web application programming interfaces (APIs).

An API is a set of specifications that allows programs to talk to one another. And a web API uses the web technologies (specifically the Hypertext Transfer Protocol, or HTTP) to allow clients to talk to servers to exchange information.

Web APIs are very useful building blocks that enable applications to get data from multiple sources. Organizations big and small can create innovation applications by leveraging the various web APIs available, all without needing to reinvent the wheel. In this chapter, I show you how to use Go to communicate with web APIs.

Without further ado, let's go!

Understanding Web APIs

Before I get to web APIs, let me get you thinking about *web applications.* You probably use web applications every day. A good example of a web application is Amazon.com. When you want to buy something at Amazon, you go to www.amazon.com and start adding items to your shopping cart. When you're done shopping, you click the button to check out and — *voilá!* — after you confirm your payment and shipping information, your items are sent to your doorstep.

Another good example of a web application is Google Finance (www.google.com/finance). If you want to check the prices of the stocks that you own, you can go to and enter the symbols of all the stocks that you're interested in. However, you may own a number of stocks — do you want to wade through pages of stocks information to find what you need? As a developer, what you probably *really* want is to aggregate all the stock information and display it in your own app so that you can have information at a glance. This is where a web API comes in.

Instead of letting people check for stock prices on Google Finance's website, Google exposes the stock data through the Google Finance API, which is designed to take in your query and return only the information you need, as shown in Figure 15-1. Often, the returning result is formatted as a JavaScript Object Notation (JSON) string, instead of HTML meant for web browsers (turn to Chapter 9 for more on JSON). Essentially, you can think of web APIs as web applications without the cool-looking user interface (UI). A web API is essentially a web application without all the bells and whistles.

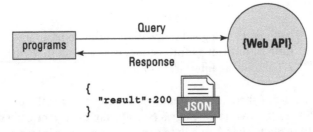

FIGURE 15-1:
A client
communicating
with a web API.

The Google Finance API is no longer maintained by Google, but there are many web APIs out there that work very much like the Google Finance API.

**TECHNICAL
STUFF**

Fetching Data from Web Services in Go

To connect to a web API, you can use the Get() function from the net/http package in Go. The Get() function accepts a URL as its argument and returns two results:

>> A Response struct

>> An error

If there is no error in connecting to the server, the error will be `nil`, and you can use the `ReadAll()` function from the `io/iotil` package to read the response from the server. The `ReadAll()` function returns two results:

>> A slice of bytes representing the response from the server

>> An error

Writing a Go program to connect to a web API

Let's write a simple Go program that connects to the Fixer web API. Fixer is a foreign exchange rates and currency conversion JSON API. Using it, you can programmatically fetch the exchange rates of various currencies. You can sign up for a free Fixer plan by going to `https://fixer.io/` and clicking the Sign Up Free button, as shown in Figure 15-2.

FIGURE 15-2:
You can sign up for free access to the Fixer API.

The free plan allows you to download the currency rates up to a thousand times per month. However, the data that is returned is only updated hourly (compared to the paid plan, in which the data may be updated as frequently as every minute). Also, the free plan has all the rates pegged to a fixed currency, the euro (€). Despite all these limitations, the Fixer API is a very good example to use when you need to connect to a web API.

After you've signed up for the free Fixer plan, you'll be given an access key together with the URL to access the API:

```
http://data.fixer.io/api/latest?access_key=<access_key>
```

The <access_key> part of the URL above will be unique to you.

After you have your access key and URL, follow these steps:

1. **Create a folder named** ConsumeWS **in your home directory:**

```
<Home>
    |__ConsumeWS
```

2. **Within the** ConsumeWS **folder, create a file named** main.go.

3. **Populate the** main.go **file with the following statements:**

```go
package main

import (
    "fmt"
    "io/ioutil"
    "log"
    "net/http"
)

func main() {
    url :=
 "http://data.fixer.io/api/latest?access_key=<access_key>"

    if resp, err := http.Get(url); err == nil {
        defer resp.Body.Close()
        if body, err := ioutil.ReadAll(resp.Body);
            err == nil {
            fmt.Println(string(body))
        } else {
            log.Fatal(err)
        }
```

```
    } else {
        log.Fatal(err)
    }
    fmt.Println("Done")
}
```

REMEMBER

Be sure to replace ‹*access_key*› with your own access key given to you by the Fixer API.

Decoding JSON data

If you've entered your Fixer API access key correctly, you should get a response from the API when you run it in the Terminal app or in Command Prompt:

```
$ cd ~/ConsumeWS
$ go run main.go
```

Examine the result returned by the web service:

```
{"success":true,"timestamp":1603847345,"base":"EUR","date"
:"2020-10-28","rates":{"AED":4.327189,"AFN":90.532761,
"ALL":123.694308,"AMD":580.987567,
...
...
"ZMK":10603.807886,"ZMW":23.900394,"ZWL":379.329977}}
```

To examine the structure of the JSON result, go to http://jsonlint.com, paste in the result, and click the Validate JSON button, shown in Figure 15-3.

The "success" key indicates whether the call to the web API succeeds. The "rates" key contains a dictionary of currency symbols and their respective rates against the base currency, the euro.

You also want to know how the JSON result will look if the call fails due to, say, an invalid API access key. In this case, you can simply change the access key in the URL to an invalid one and observe the response from the web API:

```
{"success":false,"error":{"code":101,"type":
"invalid_access_key","info":"You have not supplied a valid
API Access Key. [Technical Support:
support@apilayer.com]"}}
```

Figure 15-4 shows the structure of the JSON result when the web service call fails.

FIGURE 15-3:
Examining the structure of the JSON result returned by the Fixer API.

FIGURE 15-4:
Examining the structure of the JSON error result returned by the Fixer API.

When the structure of the result of the API is established, you can now try to *unmarshall* (decode) the JSON result to your own defined structure. You can define two structs — Result and Error — and unmarshall the result to these two structs:

```go
package main

import (
    "encoding/json"
    "fmt"
    "io/ioutil"
    "log"
    "net/http"
)

type Result struct {
    Success   bool
    Timestamp int
    Base      string
    Date      string
    Rates     map[string]float64
}

type Error struct {
    Success bool
    Error   struct {
        Code int
        Type string
        Info string
    }
}

func main() {
    url :=
        "http://data.fixer.io/api/latest?access_key=" +
        "<access_key>"

    if resp, err := http.Get(url); err == nil {
        defer resp.Body.Close()
        if body, err := ioutil.ReadAll(resp.Body); err == nil {
            var result Result
            json.Unmarshal([]byte(body), &result)
            if result.Success {
                for i, v := range result.Rates {
                    fmt.Println(i, v)
                }
```

```
          } else {
              var err Error
              json.Unmarshal([]byte(body), &err)
              fmt.Println(err.Error.Info)
          }
      } else {
          log.Fatal(err)
      }
  } else {
      log.Fatal(err)
  }
  fmt.Println("Done")
}
```

If the call is successful, you'll use the `for-range` loop to iterate through all the various currencies and their exchange rates:

```
YER 294.857281
BIF 2287.503006
FJD 2.491707
...
PKR 189.862324
TZS 2731.272293
AOA 777.187569
```

If there is an error, you'll see an error message:

```
You have not supplied a valid API Access Key. [Technical
 Support: support@apilayer.com]
```

Notice that when you print out the currencies, they aren't listed in alphabetical order. To print them in alphabetical order, you need to obtain all the keys (currencies) and sort them in alphabetical order. After the currencies are sorted, you can then use them to print out the rates:

```
if result.Success {
    // create an array to store all keys
    keys := make([]string, 0,
        len(result.Rates))

    // get all the keys---
    for k := range result.Rates {
        keys = append(keys, k)
    }
```

```
        // sort the keys
        sort.Strings(keys)

        // print the keys and values in
        // alphabetical order
        for _, k := range keys {
            fmt.Println(k, result.Rates[k])
        }

        /*
        for i, v := range result.Rates {
            fmt.Println(i, v)
        }
        */
    } else {
        var err Error
        json.Unmarshal([]byte(body), &err)
        fmt.Println(err.Error.Info)
    }
```

 You need to import the sort package to perform this sorting.

TIP

You should now see the currencies listed in alphabetical order:

```
AED 4.326224
AFN 90.731897
ALL 124.065772
...
ZMK 10601.434336
ZMW 23.992715
ZWL 379.245091
```

Refactoring the code for decoding JSON data

The code for decoding JSON data in the preceding section is good for a specific JSON structure. But if you're going to consume different web services, it would be better if you could make the decoding more generic and more flexible. Let's refactor the code into a function named fetchData():

```
func fetchData(API int) {
    url := apis[API]
    if resp, err := http.Get(url); err == nil {
```

```
        defer resp.Body.Close()
        if body, err := ioutil.ReadAll(resp.Body);
            err == nil {

            var result map[string]interface{}

            json.Unmarshal([]byte(body), &result)
            switch API {
            case 1: // for the Fixer API
                if result["success"] == true {
                    fmt.Println(result["rates"].(
                        map[string]interface{})["USD"])
                } else {
                    fmt.Println(result["error"].(
                        map[string]interface{})["info"])
                }
            }
        } else {
            log.Fatal(err)
        }
    } else {
        log.Fatal(err)
    }
}
```

The content of this fetchData() function is largely similar to the code in the preceding section, but it doesn't try to unmarshall the JSON data into a specific structure. Instead, you try to unmarshall the JSON into a map of string keys with values of type empty interface:

```
var result map[string]interface{}
```

Then, as you try to explore the details of the JSON string, you do a type assertion and extract the value based on a specific key, like the following:

```
result["rates"].(map[string]interface{})["USD"])
```

The preceding line means: Get the value for the "rates" key and then assert its value to be of type map[string] interface{}. Finally, get the value for the "USD" key. This method allows you to unmarshall JSON data of any structure without needing to define separate structs.

Also, this function takes in an integer value and uses it to reference the URL from a separate map object, which you'll define later in the `main()` function:

```
url := apis[API]
```

Based on the value of the API variable, you can then decide how you want to decode the JSON. Just add a new case in the switch statement in the code.

To put this into action, you'll consume one more web service, `http://api.openweathermap.org`. This web service has the following URL:

```
http://api.openweathermap.org/data/2.5/weather?q=SINGAPORE
&appid=<app_id>
```

The preceding URL fetches the weather information for Singapore, using the app ID that you can apply at OpenWeather (`https://home.openweathermap.org/users/sign_up`).

If the web service call succeeds, you'll get a response like this:

```
{"coord":{"lon":103.85,"lat":1.29},"weather":[{"id":501,
"main":"Rain","description":"moderate rain","icon":"10d"}]
,"base":"stations","main":{"temp":301.92,"feels_like":
306.02,"temp_min":301.15,"temp_max":302.15,"pressure":1008
,"humidity":79},"visibility":10000,"wind":{"speed":3.1,
"deg":170},"rain":{"1h":2.18},"clouds":{"all":75},"dt":
1603869175,"sys":{"type":1,"id":9470,"country":"SG",
"sunrise":1603838764,"sunset":1603882229},"timezone":
28800,"id":1880252,"name":"Singapore","cod":200}
```

Figure 15-5 shows the response as formatted by JSONLint (`https://jsonlint.com`).

If the web service call fails, you'll see the following response:

```
{"cod":401, "message": "Invalid API key. Please see
http://openweathermap.org/faq#error401 for more info."}
```

Figure 15-6 shows the formatted response.

FIGURE 15-5:
Examining the structure of the JSON result returned by the OpenWeather API.

FIGURE 15-6:
Examining the structure of the JSON error result returned by the OpenWeather API.

In the main.go file, you can now add in the following statements in bold:

```go
package main

import (
    "encoding/json"
    "fmt"
    "io/ioutil"
    "log"
    "net/http"
)

var apis map[int]string

func fetchData(API int) {
    url := apis[API]
    if resp, err := http.Get(url); err == nil {
        defer resp.Body.Close()
        if body, err := ioutil.ReadAll(resp.Body);
            err == nil {
            var result map[string]interface{}
            json.Unmarshal([]byte(body), &result)
            switch API {
            case 1:
                if result["success"] == true {
                    fmt.Println(result["rates"].(
                        map[string]interface{})["USD"])
                } else {
                    fmt.Println(result["error"].(
                        map[string]interface{})["info"])
                }
            case 2:  // for the openweathermap.org API
                if result["main"] != nil {
                    fmt.Println(result["main"].(
                        map[string]interface{})["temp"])
                } else {
                    fmt.Println(result["message"])
                }
            }
        } else {
            log.Fatal(err)
        }
    } else {
        log.Fatal(err)
```

```
        }
}

func main() {
    apis = make(map[int]string)

    apis[1] =
        "http://data.fixer.io/api/latest?access_key=" +
        "<access_key>"
    apis[2] =
        "http://api.openweathermap.org/data/2.5/weather?" +
        "q=SINGAPORE&appid=<api_key>"

    fetchData(1)
    fetchData(2)
}
```

Run the `main.go` file and notice the results returned.

Fetching from multiple web services at the same time

One of the strengths of Go is its support for concurrency. Instead of calling the two web services *sequentially* (one after the other), why not call them *concurrently* (at the same time)?

To do so, you just need to prefix each call to the `fetchData()` function with the go keyword:

```
func main() {
    apis = make(map[int]string)
    apis[1] =
        "http://data.fixer.io/api/latest?access_key=" +
        "<access_key>"
    apis[2] =
        "http://api.openweathermap.org/data/2.5/weather?" +
        "q=SINGAPORE&appid=<api_key>"

    go fetchData(1)
    go fetchData(2)

    fmt.Scanln()
}
```

Remember to call the `Scanln()` function before the end of the program. That way, the program won't exit before getting the results back from the two web service calls. Press Enter to exit the program.

Returning Goroutine's results to the main() function

So far, the results obtained from the web service have been printed out to the console. But sometimes you need to return the result from a Goroutine back to the calling function. A good way to do that is to use a *channel* (see Chapter 12). The following statements in bold show how to send data into a channel from a Goroutine, and then retrieve the data from the `main()` function:

```go
package main

import (
    "encoding/json"
    "fmt"
    "io/ioutil"
    "log"
    "net/http"
)

var apis map[int]string

// channel to store map[int]interface{}
var c chan map[int]interface{}

func fetchData(API int) {
    url := apis[API]
    if resp, err := http.Get(url); err == nil {
        defer resp.Body.Close()
        if body, err := ioutil.ReadAll(resp.Body);
            err == nil {

            var result map[string]interface{}
            json.Unmarshal([]byte(body), &result)

            var re = make(map[int]interface{})

            switch API {
            case 1:
                if result["success"] == true {
```

```go
                re[API] = result["rates"].(
                    map[string]interface{})["USD"]
            } else {
                re[API] = result["error"].(
                    map[string]interface{})["info"]
            }
            // store the result into the channel
            c <- re
            fmt.Println("Result for API 1 stored")

        case 2:
            if result["main"] != nil {
                re[API] = result["main"].(
                    map[string]interface{})["temp"]
            } else {
                re[API] = result["message"]
            }
            // store the result into the channel
            c <- re
            fmt.Println("Result for API 2 stored")
        }
    } else {
        log.Fatal(err)
    }
    } else {
        log.Fatal(err)
    }
}

func main() {

    // creates a channel to store the results from the
    // API calls
    c = make(chan map[int]interface{})

    apis = make(map[int]string)
    apis[1] =
        "http://data.fixer.io/api/latest?access_key=" +
        "<access_key>"
    apis[2] =
        "http://api.openweathermap.org/data/2.5/" +
        "weather?q=SINGAPORE&appid=<app_id>"
```

```
    go fetchData(1)
    go fetchData(2)

    // we expect two results in the channel
    for i := 0; i < 2; i++ {
        fmt.Println(<-c)
    }
    fmt.Println("Done!")

    fmt.Scanln()
}
```

Notice that you declare a channel to store map objects:

```
var c chan map[int]interface{}
```

The key for the map object is the number representing the web service you're calling (1 for the Fixer API and 2 for the OpenWeatherMap). The value for the key is the result returned by the web services. Because the result may be a string (an error message if an error occurred) or a value (if the web service succeeds), the value of the key is set to be of any type (an empty interface).

When the web APIs succeed, you should see the following results:

```
Result for API 2 stored
map[2:302.44]
Result for API 1 stored
map[1:1.175779]
Done!
```

If there is an error with the Fixer API service, the error message will be returned:

```
Result for API 2 stored
map[2:302.44]
Result for API 1 stored
map[1:You have not supplied a valid API Access Key. [Technical
   Support: support@apilayer.com]]
Done!
```

Chapter **16**

Getting Ready to Serve Using REST APIs

n Chapter 15, I explain how to consume web services using Go. But one of the strengths of Go is *server-side implementation* (back-end services such as web applications, web services, and so on) due to its strong support for concurrency programming. So, in this chapter, I show you how to use a third-party package to easily develop a web service using an architecture known as REST API.

Building Web Services Using REST APIs

When it comes to building web services, you may have heard of the term *REST*. But what exactly *is* REST and how does it really work? In this section, I explain what REST is and how you can make your web service a RESTful one.

TECHNICAL STUFF

A web service that conforms to the REST architectural style is commonly known as a *RESTful* API.

REST stands for *representational state transfer*. It's a software architectural style that defines how a web service should work and behave. REST is designed to take advantage of existing protocols. It usually uses HTTP for communicating between the client and the service.

A REST API uses several HTTP verbs for the clients to communicate with the service:

>> GET: To retrieve a resource from the service

>> PUT: To create a new resource or update an existing one on the service

>> POST: To create a new resource on the service

>> DELETE: To remove a resource from the service

A REST API can return any type of data, but most services today use JavaScript Object Notation (JSON) as the data type (for more on JSON, turn to Chapter 9). REST isn't limited to JSON, though — a REST API can also return XML, YAML, or any format that the client can understand.

In the following sections, I cover the basics of HTTP messages, what REST URLs look like, and the various methods and responses that REST supports.

HTTP messages

When communicating with a REST API, you use HTTP messages, which are made up of the following:

>> **Header:** Contains metadata, such as encoding information, HTTP methods, and so on. The header can contain only plain text. So, you cannot include non-ASCII characters in the header.

>> **Body:** Data to transmit over the network. The body can contain data in any format. The format is specified in the Content-Type field, such as Content-Type: application/json.

Figure 16-1 shows the HTTP message being sent to a web API and the response returned by it.

REST URLs

In order to communicate with a REST API, you need a URL. A REST URL identifies a resource.

HTTP Message

HTTP Header
Method: PUT
Content-Type: application/json

HTTP Body

{Web API}

Response
JSON/XML/etc

FIGURE 16-1.
Sending an HTTP
message to the
web API and the
response
returned by it.

Suppose you have a REST API that provides information on various programming courses. If you want to retrieve the information of a course using its course ID of IOS101, the URL to identify that resource would look like this:

```
http://www.yourdomain.com/api/v1/courses/IOS101
```

TIP

You're free to design your own URL, but you should stick to the conventions of a REST URL, which I outline in this section.

Figure 16-2 shows the various components that make up a REST API URL.

FIGURE 16-2:
The various
components that
make up a REST
API URL.

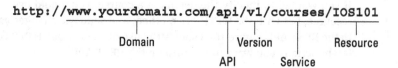

In this example, the IOS101 in the URL represents a resource. Resources are best thought of as *nouns*. Here are some examples of resources in a REST URL:

```
http://www.yourdomain.com/api/v1/customers/C12345
http://www.yourdomain.com/api/v1/titles/1119545633
http://www.yourdomain.com/api/v1/users/weimenglee
```

You should *not* use verbs in your REST API URL. For example, the following URLs should *not* be used because they all describe an action:

```
http://www.yourdomain.com/api/v1/customers/add
http://www.yourdomain.com/api/v1/titles/delete
http://www.yourdomain.com/api/v1/titles/edit
```

Use versioning in your URL so that as your API evolves, you can release new versions using a new URL without breaking clients that use your older versions of the API. For example, six months down the road, you may have a new version of your API. You may want to use a new URL for your new API:

```
http://www.yourdomain.com/api/v2/courses/IOS101
```

Using a new URL for your new API allows you to maintain multiple versions of your REST API.

REST methods

REST APIs use HTTP to communicate with the service. So, if you want to get information about a particular resource (a course, for example), you would use the following URL together with the HTTP GET method:

```
http://www.yourdomain.com/api/v1/courses/IOS101
```

If you want to get all the courses, you can use the following URL (without the resource name) with the GET method, like this:

```
http://www.yourdomain.com/api/v1/courses/
```

If you wanted to modify the details of a course, you would use the URL with the resource, but with the HTTP PUT method, and send the changes you need to make to the REST API. Figure 16-3 shows the use of the various HTTP verbs for the different actions you want to perform on the REST API.

Notice that for the PUT and POST methods, you need to send the details to the REST API. Typically, you use JSON (or other encoding formats such as XML).

Out of the four HTTP verbs, three of them are *idempotent.* Idempotent methods achieve the same result, regardless of how many times the request is repeated. GET, PUT, and DELETE are all idempotent — repeating these methods doesn't change the state of the server.

For example, suppose you send a GET method to the following URL:

```
http://www.yourdomain.com/api/v1/courses/IOS101
```

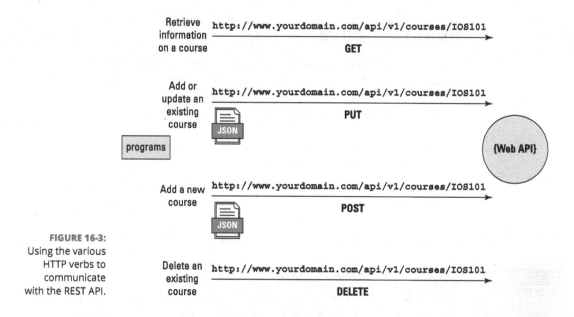

Retrieve
information
on a course

`http://www.yourdomain.com/api/v1/courses/IOS101`

GET

Add or
update an
existing
course

`http://www.yourdomain.com/api/v1/courses/IOS101`

PUT

JSON

programs

{Web API}

Add a new
course

`http://www.yourdomain.com/api/v1/courses/IOS101`

POST

JSON

FIGURE 16-3:
Using the various
HTTP verbs to
communicate
with the REST API.

Delete an
existing
course

`http://www.yourdomain.com/api/v1/courses/IOS101`

DELETE

No matter how many times you call the REST API with this URL and HTTP method, it won't alter the state of the API. Likewise, if you use the HTTP PUT verb with this URL to modify the details of a course, sending the same request the second time doesn't change the state of the REST API. The same applies to the DELETE verb — after a course is deleted, trying to delete the same course has no effect on the state of the REST API.

The POST verb, on the other hand, is *not* idempotent. When you use the HTTP POST verb, you have the option to leave out the resource. So, instead of the following URL:

```
http://www.yourdomain.com/api/v1/courses/IOS101
```

You could leave out the IOS101 when using this URL with the POST method, like this:

```
http://www.yourdomain.com/api/v1/courses/
```

The REST API will generate a new course ID whenever it receives a POST method without a resource name (this is one of the recommended behaviors of REST APIs). So, if you repeatedly use the same URL with the POST method, a new course would be created each time you make the call.

TIP

Because there is no standardized way to build REST APIs, it's really up to the individual REST APIs to decide whether they want to implement this option. For the example REST API that you build later in this chapter, you'll need a resource to be specified in the URL whenever a POST method is used.

REST response

When the REST API has received your request, it needs to perform the action that it's asked to perform, such as returning information of a course, updating it, deleting it, or adding a new course. After performing the task, the REST API needs to return the following information:

>> An HTTP response code indicating whether the operation has succeeded, failed, or otherwise

>> An optional result expected by the client, such as details on a course or a list of courses

A REST API typically returns one of the following HTTP response codes:

>> **200 OK:** The request was successful.

>> **201 Created:** The request was successful and a resource was created. This response code is used to confirm the success of a PUT or POST request.

>> **400 Bad Request:** The request was malformed. This happens especially with POST and PUT requests, when the data doesn't pass validation or is in the wrong format.

>> **404 Not Found:** The required resource couldn't be found. This response code is generally returned to all requests that point to a URL with no corresponding resource.

>> **401 Unauthorized:** You need to perform authentication before accessing the resource.

>> **405 Method Not Allowed:** The HTTP method used is not supported for this resource.

>> **409 Conflict:** A conflict has occurred — for example, you're using a POST request to create the same resource twice.

>> **500 Internal Server Error:** Generally, a 500 response is used when processing fails due to unanticipated circumstances on the server side, causing the server to error out.

REMEMBER

Because there is no standardized way to implement REST APIs, the response code returned by each REST API may vary.

Creating a REST API in Go

It's time to build a REST API yourself using Go! In this section, you create a REST API to return information about programming courses. Clients can ask for a list of courses, as well as details of a specific course. They can also add new courses, edit existing courses, and delete courses.

One easy way to build REST APIs in Go is to use the gorilla/mux package. (The name mux stands for *HTTP request multiplexer*.) The gorilla/mux package implements a request router and dispatcher for matching incoming requests to their respective handlers. Figure 16-4 shows the use of the gorilla/mux package.

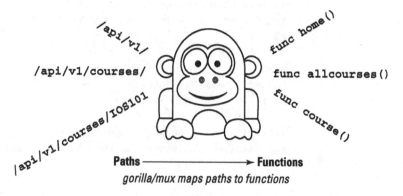

FIGURE 16-4:
Using the
gorilla/mux
package to build
REST APIs in Go.

Paths ⟶ Functions
gorilla/mux maps paths to functions

To install the gorilla/mux package, go to the Terminal application (Mac) or Command Prompt (PC), and type the following command:

```
$ go get -u github.com/gorilla/mux
```

That's it! You're ready to start coding!

Getting your REST API up and running

You're now ready to start creating your REST API. Follow these steps:

1. **Create a folder named** REST **in your home directory:**

```
<Home>
  |__REST
```

2. Within the REST **folder, create a file named** main.go.

3. Populate the main.go **file with the following statements:**

```go
package main

import (
    "fmt"
    "log"
    "net/http"
    "github.com/gorilla/mux"
)

func home(w http.ResponseWriter, r *http.Request) {
    fmt.Fprintf(w, "Welcome to the REST API!")
}

func main() {
    router := mux.NewRouter()
    router.HandleFunc("/api/v1/", home)

    fmt.Println("Listening at port 5000")
    log.Fatal(http.ListenAndServe(":5000", router))
}
```

First, you create a new instance of mux.NewRouter:

```go
router := mux.NewRouter()
```

The router instance registers routes to be matched and dispatches a handler. You then create a route (path) named "/api/vi/" and map it to the home() function:

```go
router.HandleFunc("/api/v1/", home)
```

The home() function is defined here:

```go
func home(w http.ResponseWriter, r *http.Request) {
    fmt.Fprintf(w, "Welcome to the REST API!")
}
```

The function has two parameters:

» A ResponseWriter object (from the http package) so that you can use it to construct an HTTP response to be sent back to the client

>> A pointer to a Request object (also from the http package) that represents an HTTP request sent by the client and received by the service

In this home() function, you use the Fprintf() function to send a string back to the client.

Finally, you start the REST API by listening at port 5000:

```
log.Fatal(http.ListenAndServe(":5000", router))
```

To run the REST API, type the following command in Terminal or Command Prompt:

```
$ cd ~/REST
$ go run main.go
Listening at port 5000
```

Testing the REST API

With the REST API up and running, you can now test and see if it works! You'll use the curl tool. (curl is a tool to transfer data to or from a server using one of the supported protocols, such as HTTP.)

In another Terminal or Command Prompt window, type the following command (in bold), and you should see the corresponding output:

```
$ curl http://localhost:5000/api/v1/
Welcome to the REST API!
```

If you see this, your REST API works!

Registering additional paths

Obviously, right now, this REST API isn't very useful and doesn't do much. So now let's add additional paths to the REST API so it can actually do something!

Add the following statements in bold to the main.go file:

```
package main

import (
    "fmt"
```

```go
    "log"
    "net/http"
    "github.com/gorilla/mux"
)

func home(w http.ResponseWriter, r *http.Request) {
    fmt.Fprintf(w, "Welcome to the REST API!")
}

func allcourses(w http.ResponseWriter, r *http.Request) {
    fmt.Fprintf(w, "List of all courses")
}

func course(w http.ResponseWriter, r *http.Request) {
    params := mux.Vars(r)
    fmt.Fprintf(w, "Detail for course "+params["courseid"])
}

func main() {
    router := mux.NewRouter()
    router.HandleFunc("/api/v1/", home)

    router.HandleFunc("/api/v1/courses", allcourses)
    router.HandleFunc("/api/v1/courses/{courseid}", course)

    fmt.Println("Listening at port 5000")
    log.Fatal(http.ListenAndServe(":5000", router))
}
```

Here, you're adding two more paths:

>> "/api/v1/courses" mapped to the allcourses() function

>> "/api/v1/courses/{courseid}" mapped to the course() function

Of interest is the second path — "/api/v1/courses/{courseid}". This path contains a variable enclosed within a pair of braces ({}), courseid.

In the function mapped to this path, you get hold of the value of this variable through the mux.Vars() function. This function returns the path variable(s) for the current request. It returns a value of type map[string]string. So, to get the value of the courseid variable, you use the courseid as the key to the value returned by the Vars() function:

```
func course(w http.ResponseWriter, r *http.Request) {
    params := mux.Vars(r)
    fmt.Fprintf(w, "Detail for course "
                    + params["courseid"])
}
```

Figure 16-5 summarizes how the path variables are extracted in the function.

If it's still running, stop the main.go by pressing Ctrl+C, and restart it.

Let's start to query for all courses using the following command (in another Terminal or Command Prompt window):

```
$ curl http://localhost:5000/api/v1/courses
List of all courses
```

To get the details for a particular course, use the following command:

```
$ curl http://localhost:5000/api/v1/courses/IOS101
Detail for course IOS101
```

Up to this point, you've set up the paths for obtaining details of specific courses, as well as to obtain a list of courses.

In the next section, you learn how to pass information through a path's *query string*.

TIP

A query string is the part of a URL that assigns values to specified parameters. For example, when you search for "Tokyo" on Google, the URL may look like this: www.google.com/search?q=Tokyo. The query string in this case is q=Tokyo.

Passing in query string

In the previous section, you set up the basic paths of your REST API. The paths allow you to obtain information of the course(s) that you want. Using the paths, you can also pass in additional information to the REST API through a path's query string. A path can contain a query string. A query string is useful for passing information to a service by simply embedding the information in the URL. Here's an example of a query string (it's the part in bold):

```
/api/v1/courses?country=SG&state=CA
```

A query string consists of key/value pairs (as shown in Figure 16-6).

FIGURE 16-6:
A query string
consists of key/
value pairs.

Query String

`/api/v1/courses?`country=US&state=CA

Key   Value   Key   Value

Add the following statements in bold to the allcourses() function:

```
func allcourses(w http.ResponseWriter, r *http.Request) {
    // fmt.Fprintf(w, "List of all courses")
    kv := r.URL.Query()

    for k, v := range kv {
        fmt.Println(k, v)
    }
}
```

The r.URL.Query() function returns the key/value pairs in the query string as a map object. To see each of the keys and values in the key/value pairs, you use a for-range loop.

Time to test the REST API again. If it's still running, press Ctrl+C to stop the main.go, and restart it.

In another Terminal or Command Prompt window, type the following:

```
$ curl "http://localhost:5000/api/v1/courses?
country=US&state=CA"
```

TIP

If you're typing this command on a Mac, be sure to enclose the URL with a pair of double quotes. If you don't, the & character will direct the shell to run the command in the background.

The following will be printed in the REST API window:

```
Listening at port 5000
country [US]
state [CA]
```

If you're looking for a specific key in the query string, you can use the following code snippet:

```
// check for the "country" key
if val, ok := kv["country"]; ok {
    fmt.Println(val[0])
}
```

Specifying request methods

To allow clients to query the REST API for course details, add a new course, and modify and delete existing courses, you need to configure the relevant path to support the relevant HTTP methods.

In this case, you'll use the Methods() function to specify the HTTP methods supported on a particular path:

```
func course(w http.ResponseWriter, r *http.Request) {
    params := mux.Vars(r)
    fmt.Fprintf(w, "Detail for course " +
                    params["courseid"])
    fmt.Fprintf(w, "\n")
    fmt.Fprintf(w, r.Method)
}
```

```
func main() {
    router := mux.NewRouter()
    router.HandleFunc("/api/v1/", home)

    router.HandleFunc("/api/v1/courses", allcourses)
    router.HandleFunc("/api/v1/courses/{courseid}",
                    course).Methods(
                    "GET", "PUT", "POST", "DELETE")

    fmt.Println("Listening at port 5000")
    log.Fatal(http.ListenAndServe(":5000", router))
}
```

Notice that in the `course()` function, you can know what method the path was called with using the `Method` field.

As usual, rerun the `main.go` file, and test the following using a separate Terminal or Command Prompt window:

```
$ curl http://localhost:5000/api/v1/courses/IOT201
Detail for course IOT201
GET

$ curl -X POST http://localhost:5000/api/v1/courses/IOT201
Detail for course IOT201
POST

$ curl -X PUT http://localhost:5000/api/v1/courses/IOT201
Detail for course IOT201
PUT

$ curl -X DELETE http://localhost:5000/api/v1/courses/
IOT201
Detail for course IOT201
DELETE
```

The `-X` option for the `curl` command specifies the HTTP method to use. Table 16-1 shows some of the common options available for `curl`.

TABLE 16-1 **The Various Options for curl**

Option	Purpose	Example
-X	To specify an HTTP request method	POST
-H	To specify request headers	"Content-type: application/json"
-d	To specify request data	'{"message":"Hello Data"}'
--data-binary	To specify binary request data	@file.bin
-i	To show the response headers	
-u	To specify username and password	"admin:secret"
-v	To enable verbose mode, which outputs information such as request and response headers and errors	

Storing the course information on the REST API

With all the scaffolding for our REST API done, you're now ready to write the code to store course information on the REST API. To keep things simple, you'll store the courses on your REST API using a map object.

Of course, in real-life applications, you should use a database for storing the course information. But I don't want you to be bogged down with database access codes and deviate from the more important aspects of creating the REST API.

The key of this map object is a string representing the course ID. Its value would be a struct containing a field named `Title`:

```
type courseInfo struct {
    Title string `json:"Title"`
}

var courses map[string]courseInfo
```

When the client asks for a list of all courses using the "/api/v1/courses" path, you'll JSON-encode the `courses` map object and send it back to the client using the `NewEncoder()` object's `Encode()` function:

```
func allcourses(w http.ResponseWriter, r *http.Request) {
    // fmt.Fprintf(w, "List of all courses")
    kv := r.URL.Query()
```

```
    for k, v := range kv {
        fmt.Println(k, v)
    }
    // returns all the courses in JSON
    json.NewEncoder(w).Encode(courses)
}
```

In the following sections, I walk you through how to create new courses, as well as update, retrieve, and delete courses.

Creating new courses

Things are more involved for adding new courses to the REST API. As discussed earlier, when a client wants to add a new course, the client will send a JSON string containing the details of the course. So, on the REST API, you need to check the following:

>> Check whether the "Content-type" header sent by the client is "application/ json". This is to ensure that the client is sending the correct type of content to the REST API.

>> Check the HTTP method used. If it's a POST, it's creating a new course.

>> Decode the JSON string that is sent to the REST API into the courseInfo struct.

>> After the content of the course to be added has been decoded, you need to check that the content is correct. If it isn't correct, send a 422 response code back to the client.

>> Check that the course ID doesn't already exist in the REST API. If it does, send back a 409 response code to the client.

>> Finally, add the new course to the courses map object and then send a 201 response code back to the client.

You can now add the following statements in bold to the course() and main() functions:

```
func course(w http.ResponseWriter, r *http.Request) {
    params := mux.Vars(r)

    /*
    fmt.Fprintf(w, "Detail for course " +
                params["courseid"])
```

```go
fmt.Fprintf(w, "\n")
fmt.Fprintf(w, r.Method)
*/


if r.Header.Get("Content-type")=="application/json" {

    //  POST is for creating new course
    if r.Method == "POST" {

        // read the string sent to the service
        var newCourse courseInfo
        reqBody, err := ioutil.ReadAll(r.Body)

        if err == nil {
            // convert JSON to object
            json.Unmarshal(reqBody, &newCourse)

            if newCourse.Title == "" {
                w.WriteHeader(
                    http.StatusUnprocessableEntity)
                w.Write([]byte(
                    "422 - Please supply course " +
                    "information " + "in JSON format"))
                return
            }

            // check if course exists; add only if
            // course does not exist
            if _, ok := courses[params["courseid"]];
                !ok {
                courses[params["courseid"]] =
                    newCourse
                w.WriteHeader(http.StatusCreated)
                w.Write([]byte("201 - Course added: "
                    + params["courseid"]))
            } else {
                w.WriteHeader(http.StatusConflict)
                w.Write([]byte(
                    "409 - Duplicate course ID"))
            }
        } else {
            w.WriteHeader(
                http.StatusUnprocessableEntity)
            w.Write([]byte("422 - Please supply course
information " + "in JSON format"))
```

```
            }
          }
        }
      }
func main() {
    // instantiate courses
    courses = make(map[string]courseInfo)

    router := mux.NewRouter()
    router.HandleFunc("/api/v1/", home)

    router.HandleFunc("/api/v1/courses", allcourses)
    router.HandleFunc("/api/v1/courses/{courseid}", course).
  Methods("GET", "PUT", "POST", "DELETE")

    fmt.Println("Listening at port 5000")
    log.Fatal(http.ListenAndServe(":5000", router))
}
```

Updating courses

The next operation you need to implement is updating existing courses. The process for updating existing courses is very similar to that of adding new courses. The key difference is that for updating courses, the client will use the PUT method instead of the POST method.

You need to perform the following checks:

» Check if the client uses the PUT method.

» Decode the JSON string that is sent to the REST API into the courseInfo struct.

» Check whether the course ID already exists. If it does not already exist, add the new course to the courses map object. Otherwise, update the existing course.

You can now add the following statements in bold to the course() function:

```
func course(w http.ResponseWriter, r *http.Request) {
    params := mux.Vars(r)


    if r.Header.Get("Content-type")=="application/json" {
```

```go
//---POST is for creating new course---
if r.Method == "POST" {
    ...
}


//---PUT is for creating or updating
// existing course---
if r.Method == "PUT" {
    var newCourse courseInfo
    reqBody, err := ioutil.ReadAll(r.Body)

    if err == nil {
        json.Unmarshal(reqBody, &newCourse)

        if newCourse.Title == "" {
            w.WriteHeader(
                http.StatusUnprocessableEntity)
            w.Write([]byte(
                "422 - Please supply course " +
                " information " +
                "in JSON format"))
            return
        }

        // check if course exists; add only if
        // course does not exist
        if _, ok := courses[params["courseid"]];
            !ok {
            courses[params["courseid"]] =
                newCourse
            w.WriteHeader(http.StatusCreated)
            w.Write([]byte("201 - Course added: "
                            + params["courseid"]))
        } else {
            // update course
            courses[params["courseid"]] =
                newCourse
            w.WriteHeader(http.StatusNoContent)
        }
    } else {
        w.WriteHeader(
            http.StatusUnprocessableEntity)
        w.Write([]byte("422 - Please supply " +
                    "course information " +
                    "in JSON format"))
```

```
        }
      }
    }
  }
```

Retrieving courses

The client can also fetch a specific course using the GET method with the following path:

```
/api/v1/courses/<course_id>
```

To return the specified course, you just need to check whether the client uses the GET method. You then return the course if it exists, or return a response of 404 if the course does not exist:

```go
func course(w http.ResponseWriter, r *http.Request) {
    params := mux.Vars(r)

    if r.Method == "GET" {
        if _, ok := courses[params["courseid"]]; ok {
            json.NewEncoder(w).Encode(
                courses[params["courseid"]])
        } else {
            w.WriteHeader(http.StatusNotFound)
            w.Write([]byte("404 - No course found"))
        }
    }

    if r.Header.Get("Content-type")=="application/json" {

        //---POST is for creating new course---
        if r.Method == "POST" {
            ...
        }

        //---PUT is for creating or updating
        // existing course---
        if r.Method == "PUT" {
            ...
        }
    }
}
```

Deleting courses

The last operation you need to implement is deleting a course. The first thing you check is whether the client sends a DELETE method. Then you try to delete the course if it already exists, or return a 404 error if there is no such course:

```go
func course(w http.ResponseWriter, r *http.Request) {
    params := mux.Vars(r)

    if r.Method == "GET" {
        ...
    }

    if r.Method == "DELETE" {
        if _, ok := courses[params["courseid"]]; ok {
            delete(courses, params["courseid"])
            w.WriteHeader(http.StatusNoContent)
        } else {
            w.WriteHeader(http.StatusNotFound)
            w.Write([]byte("404 - No course found"))
        }
    }

    if r.Header.Get("Content-type")=="application/json" {

        //---POST is for creating new course---
        if r.Method == "POST" {
            ...
        }

        //---PUT is for creating or updating
        // existing course---
        if r.Method == "PUT" {
            ...
        }
    }
}
```

With these additions, this is how the final main.go file looks:

```go
package main

import (
    "encoding/json"
    "fmt"
```

```go
    "io/ioutil"
    "log"
    "net/http"
    "github.com/gorilla/mux"
)

type courseInfo struct {
    Title string `json:"Title"`
}

var courses map[string]courseInfo

func home(w http.ResponseWriter, r *http.Request) {
    fmt.Fprintf(w, "Welcome to the REST API!")
}

func allcourses(w http.ResponseWriter, r *http.Request) {
    kv := r.URL.Query()

    for k, v := range kv {
        fmt.Println(k, v)
    }
    // returns all the courses in JSON
    json.NewEncoder(w).Encode(courses)
}

func course(w http.ResponseWriter, r *http.Request) {
    params := mux.Vars(r)

    if r.Method == "GET" {
        if _, ok := courses[params["courseid"]]; ok {
            json.NewEncoder(w).Encode(
                courses[params["courseid"]])
        } else {
            w.WriteHeader(http.StatusNotFound)
            w.Write([]byte("404 - No course found"))
        }
    }

    if r.Method == "DELETE" {
        if _, ok := courses[params["courseid"]]; ok {
            delete(courses, params["courseid"])
            w.WriteHeader(http.StatusNoContent)
        } else {
```

```go
            w.WriteHeader(http.StatusNotFound)
            w.Write([]byte("404 - No course found"))
        }
    }

    if r.Header.Get("Content-type")=="application/json" {

        // POST is for creating new course
        if r.Method == "POST" {
            // read the string sent to the service
            var newCourse courseInfo
            reqBody, err := ioutil.ReadAll(r.Body)

            if err == nil {
                // convert JSON to object
                json.Unmarshal(reqBody, &newCourse)

                if newCourse.Title == "" {
                    w.WriteHeader(
                        http.StatusUnprocessableEntity)
                    w.Write([]byte(
                        "422 - Please supply course " +
                        "information in JSON format"))
                    return
                }

                // check if course exists; add only if
                // course does not exist
                if _, ok := courses[params["courseid"]];
                    !ok {
                    courses[params["courseid"]] =
                        newCourse
                    w.WriteHeader(http.StatusCreated)
                    w.Write([]byte("201 - Course added: "
                                    + params["courseid"]))
                } else {
                    w.WriteHeader(http.StatusConflict)
                    w.Write([]byte(
                        "409 - Duplicate course ID"))
                }
            } else {
                w.WriteHeader(
                    http.StatusUnprocessableEntity)
                w.Write([]byte("422 - Please supply " +
                    "course information in JSON format"))
```

```go
        }
    }

    //---PUT is for creating or updating existing
    // course---
    if r.Method == "PUT" {
        var newCourse courseInfo
        reqBody, err := ioutil.ReadAll(r.Body)

        if err == nil {
            json.Unmarshal(reqBody, &newCourse)

            if newCourse.Title == "" {
                w.WriteHeader(
                    http.StatusUnprocessableEntity)
                w.Write([]byte("422 - Please supply" +
                " course information in JSON format"))
                return
            }

            // check if course exists; add only if
            // course does not exist
            if _, ok := courses[params["courseid"]];
                !ok {
                courses[params["courseid"]] =
                    newCourse
                w.WriteHeader(http.StatusCreated)
                w.Write([]byte("201 - Course added: "
                    + params["courseid"]))
            } else {
                // update course
                courses[params["courseid"]] =
                    newCourse
                w.WriteHeader(http.StatusNoContent)
            }
        } else {
            w.WriteHeader(
                http.StatusUnprocessableEntity)
            w.Write([]byte("422 - Please supply " +
                "course information in JSON format"))
        }
    }
}
```

```
func main() {
    // instantiate courses
    courses = make(map[string]courseInfo)

    router := mux.NewRouter()
    router.HandleFunc("/api/v1/", home)

    router.HandleFunc("/api/v1/courses", allcourses)
    router.HandleFunc("/api/v1/courses/{courseid}", course).
  Methods("GET", "PUT", "POST", "DELETE")

    fmt.Println("Listening at port 5000")
    log.Fatal(http.ListenAndServe(":5000", router))
}
```

Testing the REST API again

Now you're ready to test the REST API again. First, make sure you run the main. go program:

```
$ go run main.go
Listening at port 5000
```

In Terminal or Command Prompt, check for all the courses in the REST API:

```
$ curl http://localhost:5000/api/v1/courses
{}
```

The preceding output shows that there are no courses at this moment. Next, let's add a new course with the course ID IOS101 and title "iOS Programming" using the POST method:

```
$ curl -H "Content-Type:application/json" -X POST
http://localhost:5000/api/v1/courses/IOS101 -d
"{\"title\":\"iOS Programming\"}"
201 - Course added: IOS101
```

The output shows that the course has now been added. If you try to issue the preceding command again, you'll see the output shown below:

```
$ curl -H "Content-Type:application/json" -X POST
http://localhost:5000/api/v1/courses/IOS101 -d
```

```
"{\"title\":\"iOS Programming\"}"
409 - Duplicate course ID
```

Because the course already exists, you'll get the 409 error.

Now try to get all the courses in the REST API:

```
$ curl http://localhost:5000/api/v1/courses
{"IOS101":{"Title":"iOS Programming"}}
```

So far so good. At this point, there is one course in the REST API. Let's now add a new course, IOS102, using the PUT method:

```
$ curl -H "Content-Type: application/json" -X PUT
http://localhost:5000/api/v1/courses/IOS102 -d
"{\"title\":\"Swift Programming\"}"
201 - Course added: IOS102
```

Next, let's change the title of the course that we've just added by using the same PUT method, but with the course title changed:

```
$ curl -H "Content-Type: application/json" -X PUT
http://localhost:5000/api/v1/courses/IOS102 -d
"{\"title\":\"SwiftUI Programming\"}"
```

TIP

HTTP response code 204 indicates that the server has successfully fulfilled the request and that there is no content to send in the response payload body.

This time, there is no reply from the server. So, let's verify that the course title has, indeed, been changed:

```
$ curl http://localhost:5000/api/v1/courses
{"IOS101":{"Title":"iOS Programming"},
"IOS102":{"Title":"SwiftUI Programming"}}
```

The reply confirms that the title has been changed. You can also try fetching the specific course:

```
$ curl http://localhost:5000/api/v1/courses/IOS102
{"Title":"SwiftUI Programming"}
```

Now try deleting the IOS102 course:

```
$ curl -X DELETE
http://localhost:5000/api/v1/courses/IOS102
```

Again, the server actually responded with 204, so there is no output here. Let's try to query for IOS102:

```
$ curl http://localhost:5000/api/v1/courses/IOS102
404 - No course found
```

The output confirmed that the course was successfully deleted. Finally, let's query the API again to see the full list of courses:

```
$ curl http://localhost:5000/api/v1/courses
{"IOS101":{"Title":"iOS Programming"}}
```

You've now successfully built a functioning REST API! Congratulations!

Chapter **17**

Working with Databases

A ny application worth its salt needs to store its data persistently somewhere. Unless you're writing a "Hello, World!" application, chances are, your application will deal with data. You need a place to store that data efficiently so you can retrieve it easily the next time you need to access it.

When it comes to database servers, you have lots of choices. Here are some of the popular database servers currently available:

» IBM Db2

» Microsoft SQL Server

» MongoDB

» MySQL

» Oracle Database

» PostgreSQL

Although Go can access any of these database servers, I can't cover all these products in this chapter, so I focus on MySQL because it's one of the more popular databases for web-based applications.

In this chapter, I show you how to use Go to store your data in databases. You discover how to set up a MySQL database server, create a database and table, and configure it for use with Go.

Setting Up a MySQL Database Server

MySQL has several paid editions designed for commercial use, but you can use the free version, MySQL Community Server, for both development and commercial use. The free version has all the features that you would expect from a database server, such as the ability to create tables, views, triggers, and stored procedures (you just have to pay for technical support if you need it). MySQL Community Server is the database of choice for organizations on a tight budget.

You can download it here:

» **macOS:** https://dev.mysql.com/downloads/file/?id=499568

» **Windows:** https://dev.mysql.com/downloads/file/?id=499590

After you've downloaded the MySQL Community Server installer, run it and follow the various installation steps. Toward the end of the installation process, you're asked to provide a password for the *root account* (the user account that has all the privileges in all the MySQL databases). Be sure to provide a secure password for the root account.

In the following sections, I explain how to:

» Interface with the MySQL server

» Create a database and a table

» Create a user account and grant it permission to access the database and table

Interfacing with the MySQL server

There are a couple of ways to interface with the MySQL server. You can use the command-line utility mysql, or you can use MySQL Workbench (see Figure 17-1), which is a graphical user interface (GUI) application.

TIP

The MySQL installer for Windows automatically installs both the mysql utility and the MySQL Workbench app. Mac users need to manually download MySQL Workbench from https://dev.mysql.com/downloads/file/?id=498743.

If you're not a fan of typing commands in Terminal or Command Prompt, MySQL Workbench makes interfacing with MySQL less intimidating. But for this chapter, I show you how to interface with MySQL using the mysql utility.

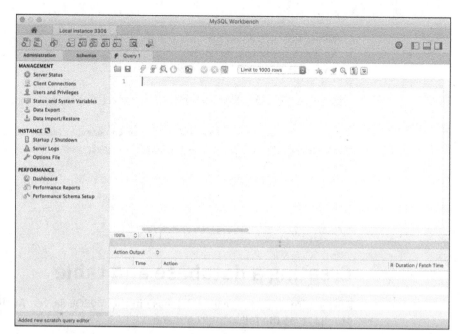

In Terminal/Command Prompt, type the following command:

```
$ mysql -u root -p
Enter password: <password>
```

Enter the password for the root account.

TIP

If you get an error that says the mysql utility is not found, the path to the utility isn't set correctly, but you can fix that problem. Here's how:

>> If you're on a Mac, type the following command:

```
export PATH=$PATH:/usr/local/mysql/bin
```

>> If you're using Windows, type the following command (verify that the directory below exists on your computer):

```
Set PATH=%PATH%;"C:\Program Files\MySQL\MySQL Server 8.0\
    bin\"
```

If you've entered the correct root password, you should see the following MySQL client prompt:

```
Welcome to the MySQL monitor.  Commands end with ; or \g.
Your MySQL connection id is 69
Server version: 8.0.17 MySQL Community Server - GPL

Copyright (c) 2000, 2020, Oracle and/or its affiliates. All rights reserved.

Oracle is a registered trademark of Oracle Corporation and/or its
affiliates. Other names may be trademarks of their respective
owners.

Type 'help;' or '\h' for help. Type '\c' to clear the current input statement.

mysql>
```

Creating a database and table

Now you're ready to create a database in the MySQL server. At the MySQL client prompt, type the following command:

```
mysql> CREATE DATABASE CoursesDB;
Query OK, 1 row affected (0.01 sec)
```

The preceding output indicates that the database CoursesDB has been created.

A number of databases are installed by default in the MySQL server, so you need to tell MySQL server which database you want to use. To do that, use the following command:

```
mysql> USE CoursesDB;
Database changed
```

Now create a table within the CoursesDB database:

```
mysql> CREATE TABLE Course (ID varchar(6) NOT NULL PRIMARY KEY,
    Details VARCHAR(100));
Query OK, 0 rows affected (0.05 sec)
```

The preceding command creates a table named Course with two columns: ID and Details. The ID column serves as the primary key for the table, and it can accept string values up to six characters. The Details column can accept string values up to 100 characters.

With the table created, you can now try to insert a record into the table using the following command:

```
mysql> INSERT INTO Course (ID, Details) VALUES
   ("IOT210","Applied Go Programming");
Query OK, 1 row affected (0.01 sec)
```

Finally, you want to verify that the record was, indeed, inserted into the table by retrieving it:

```
mysql> SELECT * FROM Course;
+--------+------------------------+
| ID     | Details                |
+--------+------------------------+
| IOT210 | Applied Go Programming |
+--------+------------------------+
1 row in set (0.00 sec)
```

If you see this output, the record has been inserted successfully.

Creating a new account and granting permission

After your database and table have been created, you're ready to create a user account so you can use it to access the database from your Go program.

WARNING

Technically, you can use the root account to access the database and table, but that isn't a good idea. Usually, you want to create separate user accounts to access specific databases and tables. The root account has the power to do anything to your databases (including deleting them), so it's better to create separate accounts with the privileges they need to do their work. That way, if a user account is compromised, the vulnerability is only limited to some specific databases and tables.

In the MySQL client utility, enter the following command:

```
mysql> CREATE USER 'gouser'@'localhost' IDENTIFIED BY
   'password';
Query OK, 0 rows affected (0.06 sec)
```

The preceding statement creates a user account named *gouser* with the specified password (which, for this example, is just *password*) and restricts its access to the localhost (meaning this account can access MySQL server only from the same machine as the server).

Obviously, for real-world usage, you would never use such a simple password.

With the user account created, the next thing to do is to grant the account the required permission to access a particular database and table. To grant the account permission to access all databases and tables in the MySQL server, type the following command:

```
mysql> GRANT ALL ON *.* TO 'gouser'@'localhost';
Query OK, 0 rows affected (0.02 sec)
```

The preceding statement grants the gouser account access privileges to all the databases and tables available on the server. To only grant the gouser account access to the Course table in the CoursesDB database and tables, specify the database and table names, like this:

```
mysql> GRANT ALL ON CoursesDB.Course TO 'gouser'@'localhost';
```

Connecting to the MySQL Database in Go

With the MySQL Server configured with the database and user account, you can finally focus on getting your Go program to talk to the database server.

Go provides a SQL database application programming interface (API) in its standard library database/sql package. However, the specific driver for the database server must be installed separately. This implementation allows developers to use a uniform API while at the same time being able to use different database servers.

To work with the MySQL server in your Go application, you can install the mysql driver by using this command in Terminal/Command Prompt:

```
$ go get "github.com/go-sql-driver/mysql"
```

To work with the standard SQL API, you just need to import the database/sql package, as well as the package for the driver of the database server that you're using. For example, in this chapter, I'm using the MySQL server, so the import looks like this:

```
import (
    "database/sql"
    _ "github.com/go-sql-driver/mysql"
)
```

The underscore character (_) prefixing the second import statement is known as the *blank identifier*. Its use is to import the specified package solely for its side effects. In this case, the mysql package registers itself with the database/sql package during the import phase, so that by the time the code in main() is executed, the database/sql package knows that it's working with a MySQL database.

You can now try to connect to the MySQL server with the following program:

```go
package main

import (
    "database/sql"
    "fmt"
    _ "github.com/go-sql-driver/mysql"
)

func main() {
    // Use mysql as driverName and a valid DSN
    db, err := sql.Open("mysql",
        "gouser:password@tcp(127.0.0.1:3306)/CoursesDB")

    // handle error
    if err != nil {
        panic(err.Error())
    } else {
        fmt.Println("Database object created")
    }

    // defer the close till after the main function has
    // finished executing
    defer db.Close()
}
```

The first argument to the sql.Open() function specifies the type of database server you're connecting to ("mysql" for MySQL). The second argument is a data source name (DSN) indicating the following:

» User account

» Password

» IP address of the database server

» Port number of the database server

» Database name

The DSN has the following format:

```
<user>:<password>@tcp(<ip_address>:<port>)/<DB_name>
```

Be aware that the sql.Open() function only creates a DB object — it doesn't yet open any connection. So, even if your username or password is wrong, you won't get an error until you try to query the database. If an error occurred when trying to create the DB object, the sql.Open() function returns the error through the second return value of the function.

Finally, notice that you'll close the database connection before the main() function exits.

In the following sections, I show you how to perform create–retrieve–update–delete (CRUD) operations on the table.

Retrieving a record

Let's now try to retrieve the record that is already in the Course table from the CoursesDB database. The statements in bold do the following:

>> Create a type called Course with two fields: ID and Details.

>> Define a function named Records to fetch records from the database and then print them out.

```go
package main

import (
    "database/sql"
    "fmt"

    _ "github.com/go-sql-driver/mysql"
)

// map this type to the record in the table
type Course struct {
    ID      string
    Details string
}

func GetRecords(db *sql.DB) {
    results, err := db.Query("Select * FROM Course")
```

```go
        if err != nil {
            panic(err.Error())
        }

        for results.Next() {
            // map this type to the record in the table
            var course Course
            err = results.Scan(&course.ID,
                &course.Details)
            if err != nil {
                panic(err.Error())
            }

            fmt.Println(course.ID,
                "-", course.Details)
        }
    }

func main() {
    // Use mysql as driverName and a valid DSN
    db, err := sql.Open("mysql",
        "gouser:password@tcp(127.0.0.1:3306)/CoursesDB")

    // handle error
    if err != nil {
        panic(err.Error())
    } else {
        fmt.Println("Database object created")
        GetRecords(db)
    }

    // defer the close till after the main function has
    // finished executing
    defer db.Close()
}
```

You use the Query() function to perform a query on the table. You usually use the Query() function to execute queries that return rows. This function returns a Rows struct containing the result of the query, as well as an error (if there is one). The cursor starts before the first row of the result set. You have to use the Next() method to move from one row to another. For each row, you use the Scan() method from the Rows struct to read the records from the table and map it to the fields in the Course struct that you've defined.

Now when you run the earlier program, you see the following output:

```
$ go run main.go
Database object created
IOT210 - Applied Go Programming
```

If you see this output, congratulations! You're now able to access the MySQL server. If you don't see this output, double-check that the database username and password are correct and that you have a database named CoursesDB in your local MySQL server.

Adding a record

When you're able to retrieve rows from your table, you're ready to write the code to insert new records into the table. The following function, InsertRecord(), does just that:

```
func InsertRecord(db *sql.DB, ID string, Details string) {
    // use parameterized SQL statement
    result, err := db.Exec(
      "INSERT INTO Course VALUES (?, ?)", ID, Details)
    if err != nil {
        fmt.Println(err.Error())
    } else {
        if count, err := result.RowsAffected(); err == nil {
            fmt.Println(count, "row(s) affected")
        }
    }
}
```

To insert a record into the table, you use the Exec() function, which executes a query without returning any rows. The second argument of the Exec() function contains the values to pass into the query's placeholders (indicated with the ? characters). This is known as a *parameterized SQL statement*. Although this function doesn't return any rows, it returns a Result struct. Using the result, you can determine if the record is inserted successfully using the RowsAffected() method.

TIP

If you need to know the ID of the row inserted, you can use the LastInsertId() method of the Result struct. This typically works for tables that have an auto-increment column for new rows that are inserted.

Now I'll insert a new course, IOS101, to the table by calling the `InsertRecord()` function:

```go
func main() {
    // Use mysql as driverName and a valid DSN
    db, err := sql.Open("mysql",
        "gouser:password@tcp(127.0.0.1:3306)/CoursesDB")

    // handle error
    if err != nil {
        panic(err.Error())
    } else {
        fmt.Println("Database object created")
        InsertRecord(db, "IOS101", "iOS Programming")
        GetRecords(db)
    }

    // defer the close till after the main function has
    // finished executing
    defer db.Close()
}
```

When you now run the program, you see the newly inserted record printed out:

```
$ go run main.go
Database object created
1 row(s) affected
IOS101 - iOS Programming
IOT210 - Applied Go Programming
```

Modifying a record

The next step would be to modify an existing record in the table. To do that, define the `EditRecord()` function as follows:

```go
func EditRecord(db *sql.DB, ID string, Details string) {
    result, err := db.Exec(
        "UPDATE Course SET Details=? WHERE ID=?",
        Details, ID)
    if err != nil {
        fmt.Println(err.Error())
```

```
    } else {
        if count, err := result.RowsAffected();
            err == nil {
            fmt.Println(count, "row(s) affected")
        }
    }
}
```

Like the previous section, you used the Exec() function to execute the SQL query to modify an existing record. To know if the record is modified successfully, use the RowsAffected() method.

The following statements calls the EditRecord() function to edit the details of the IOS101 course:

```
func main() {
    // Use mysql as driverName and a valid DSN
    db, err := sql.Open("mysql",
        "gouser:password@tcp(127.0.0.1:3306)/CoursesDB")

    // handle error
    if err != nil {
        panic(err.Error())
    } else {
        fmt.Println("Database object created")
        // InsertRecord(db, "IOS101", "iOS Programming")
        EditRecord(db, "IOS101", "SwiftUI Programming")
        GetRecords(db)
    }

    // defer the close till after the main function has finished
  executing
    defer db.Close()
}
```

The following result shows that the course has been modified correctly:

```
$ go run main.go
Database object created
1 row(s) affected
IOS101 - SwiftUI Programming
IOT210 - Applied Go Programming
```

Deleting a record

Finally, let's define the DeleteRecord() function as follows to delete a record from the table:

```
func DeleteRecord(db *sql.DB, ID string) {
    result, err := db.Exec(
        "DELETE FROM Course WHERE ID=?", ID)
    if err != nil {
        fmt.Println(err.Error())
    } else {
        if count, err := result.RowsAffected();
            err == nil {
            fmt.Println(count, "row(s) affected")
        }
    }
}
```

Just like modifying an existing record and inserting a new record, you can use the Exec() method to delete an existing record. To know if the record has been successfully deleted, check the RowsAffected() method.

I'll now delete the IOS101 course by adding the following statements in bold to the main() function:

```
func main() {
    // Use mysql as driverName and a valid DSN
    db, err := sql.Open("mysql",
        "gouser:password@tcp(127.0.0.1:3306)/CoursesDB")

    // handle error
    if err != nil {
        panic(err.Error())
    } else {
        fmt.Println("Database object created")
        // InsertRecord(db, "IOS101", "iOS Programming")
        // EditRecord(db, "IOS101", "SwiftUI Programming")
        DeleteRecord(db, "IOS101")
        GetRecords(db)
    }

    // defer the close till after the main function has finished
    executing
    defer db.Close()
}
```

When you run the program, you see the following output:

```
$ go run main.go
Database object created
1 row(s) affected
IOT210 - Applied Go Programming
```

6

The Part of Tens

IN THIS PART . . .

Discover ten Go packages to create compelling applications.

Find ten Go resources to make you a better Go developer.

Chapter **18**

Ten Useful Go Packages to Create Applications

G o comes with various standard libraries that enable you to accomplish most of the tasks you need to perform. However, sometimes you need more than what the standard library offers. Fortunately, thanks to the vibrant Go developer community, chances are, the functionalities you need are already fulfilled by one or more of the third-party packages available. So, instead of reinventing the wheel and writing the code yourself, you can simply download the package and use it in your program. In this chapter, I introduce ten packages that you may find useful in your application.

color

Tired of the boring black-and-white command-line applications? Inject some life into your Go command-line app using the `color` package. With the `color` package, you can use different colors in your app to highlight important messages or errors.

Installation

```
$ go get github.com/fatih/color
```

Code sample

```
package main

import "github.com/fatih/color"

func main() {
    color.Red("Error Message")
    color.Green("Retro...")
    color.Blue("Color is cool!")
    customBg :=
        color.New(color.FgBlue).Add(
            color.BgWhite).Add(color.Italic)
    customBg.Println("How does this look like?")
}
```

now

Anyone who has worked with date and time knows that it's a pain in the you know what. The now package is a time toolkit for Golang that wraps around the standard time package and makes dealing with date and time a little more pleasant.

Installation

```
$ go get github.com/jinzhu/now
```

Code sample

```
package main

import (
    "fmt"
    "time"

    "github.com/jinzhu/now"
)
```

```
func main() {
    fmt.Println(time.Now().Date())
    // 2020 December 8

    fmt.Println(now.Monday().Date())
    // 2020 December 7

    fmt.Println(now.BeginningOfWeek().Date())
    // 2020 December 6

    fmt.Println(now.EndOfWeek().Date())
    // 2020 December 12

    t, err := now.Parse("2020-12-13")
    if err == nil {
        fmt.Println(t)
        // 2020-12-13 00:00:00 +0800 +08
    }
}
```

go-pushbullet

If you want to send your own custom push notifications to your Android phone or web browser, but you don't want to write your own custom app to receive them, the Pushbullet app (www.pushbullet.com) is your best friend. Pushbullet is an application that runs on Android devices and Windows machines, as well as the Chrome and Firefox web browsers. After you've installed it, you can send your own custom push notifications to all these devices. Pushbullet is a great choice for building Internet of Things (IoT) apps. To send push notifications to the Pushbullet apps, you can use the go-pushbullet package.

Installation

```
$ go get github.com/xconstruct/go-pushbullet
```

Code sample

```
package main

import (
```

```
    "fmt"
    "os"
    "github.com/xconstruct/go-pushbullet"
)

func main() {

    fmt.Println(os.Args)

    pb := pushbullet.New("<access_token>")
    devs, err := pb.Devices()
    if err != nil {
        panic(err)
    } else {
        err := pb.PushNote(devs[0].Iden, os.Args[1], os.Args[2])
        if err != nil {
            panic(err)
        }
    }
}
```

goid

You may need to generate universally unique identifiers (UUIDs). For example, when you build a representation state transfer (REST) application programming interface (API), you need to provide access keys to your users who are going to access your APIs. Usually, you use a UUID as the access key. To programmatically generate a UUID in Go, you can use the goid package, which generates V4 UUIDs.

Installation

```
$ go get github.com/jakehl/goid
```

Code sample

```
package main

import (
    "fmt"
```

```
        "github.com/jakehl/goid"
)

func main() {
    fmt.Println(goid.NewV4UUID())
    // e64aedea-4aa6-4afe-8aea-d0ec068f1b3a
}
```

json2go

Converting JavaScript Object Notation (JSON) to Go structs is a straightforward task — unless the JSON content is nested and complex. This is where json2go comes in handy. The json2go package can be used directly in a command line or from a Go application.

Installation

```
$ go get github.com/m-zajac/json2go/...
```

Code sample

```
package main

import (
    "fmt"

    "github.com/m-zajac/json2go"
)

func main() {
    inputs :=
        `[
            {
                "name": "water",
                "type": "liquid",
                "boiling_point": {
                    "units": "C",
                    "value": 100
                }
            },
```

```
            {
                "name": "carbon monoxide",
                "type": "gas",
                "dangerous": true,
                "boiling_point": {
                    "units": "C",
                    "value": -191.5
                },
                "density": {
                    "units": "kg/m3",
                    "value": 789
                }
            }
        ]`
    parser := json2go.NewJSONParser("Document")
    parser.FeedBytes([]byte(inputs))
    res := parser.String()
    fmt.Println(res)
    /*
        type Document []struct {
            BoilingPoint struct {
                    Units string `json:"units"`
                    Value float64 `json:"value"`
            } `json:"boiling_point"`
            Dangerous *bool `json:"dangerous,omitempty"`
            Density   *struct {
                    Units string `json:"units"`
                    Value int    `json:"value"`
            } `json:"density,omitempty"`
            Name string `json:"name"`
            Type string `json:"type"`
        }
    */
}
```

gojq

In Go, you can decode JSON strings using the UnMarshal() function from the json package. However, that requires you to *unmarshal* (decode) the JSON string into a Go struct or onto an empty interface (for unstructured JSON). What if you just want to very quickly parse some JSON configuration string, and you don't want to

get your hands dirty doing things like type assertion? The answer: Use the
gojq package. The gojq package allows you to quickly extract values from a JSON
string.

Installation

```
$ go get github.com/elgs/gojq
```

Code sample

```
package main

import (
    "fmt"

    "github.com/elgs/gojq"
)

func main() {
    inputs :=
        `[
            {
                "name": "water",
                "type": "liquid",
                "boiling_point": {
                    "units": "C",
                    "value": 100
                }
            },
            {
                "name": "carbon monoxide",
                "type": "gas",
                "dangerous": true,
                "features":[
                    {
                        "type":"boiling_point",
                        "units":"C",
                        "value":-191.5
                    },
                    {
                        "type":"density",
                        "units":"kg/m3",
                        "value":789
```

```
                }
            ]
        }
    ]`

    parser, err := gojq.NewStringQuery(inputs)
    if err != nil {
        fmt.Println(err)
        return
    }
    fmt.Println(parser.Query("[0].name"))
    // water

    fmt.Println(parser.Query("[1].features.[0].type"))
    // boiling_point

    fmt.Println(parser.Query("[1].features.[0].units"))
    // C

    fmt.Println(parser.Query("[1].features.[1].value"))
    // 789
}
```

turtle

Want to make your Go program resonate with kids? Well, talk to them using emojis! The turtle package allows you to inject emojis into your Go application. You'll be able to get emojis by name or look them up by name.

Installation

```
$ go get github.com/hackebrot/turtle
```

Code sample

```
package main

import (
    "fmt"
    "os"
```

```
        "github.com/hackebrot/turtle"
)

func main() {
    name := "happy"
    emojis := turtle.Keyword(name)
    if emojis == nil {
        fmt.Fprintf(os.Stderr, "no emoji found for name: %v\n",
            name)
        os.Exit(1)
    }
    fmt.Printf("%s: %s\n", name, emojis)
}
```

go-http-client

Often, you want to connect to a web server and fetch some data quickly. You can use the `go-http-client` package to do just that.

Installation

```
$ go get github.com/bozd4g/go-http-client/
```

Code sample

```
package main

import (
    "fmt"

    client "github.com/bozd4g/go-http-client"
)

func main() {
    httpClient := client.New(
        "https://jsonplaceholder.typicode.com/")
    if request, err := httpClient.Get("posts/10");
        err != nil {
        panic(err)
    } else {
```

```
        if response, err := httpClient.Do(request);
            err != nil {
            panic(err)
        } else {
            fmt.Println(string(response.Get().Body))
        }
    }
}
```

notify

The notify package allows you to monitor changes to your file systems. For example, you may want to be notified whenever a file or folder has been created, deleted, or renamed in a particular folder. The notify package abstracts all the lower-level filesystem watchers like inotify, kqueue, FSEvents, FEN, or ReadDirectoryChangesW.

Installation

```
$ go get github.com/rjeczalik/notify
```

Code sample

```
package main

import (
    "log"

    "github.com/rjeczalik/notify"
)

func main() {
    for {
        c := make(chan notify.EventInfo, 1)

        // monitor the current directory for file/folder
        // creation, deletion, and renaming
        if err := notify.Watch(".", c, notify.Create,
            notify.Remove, notify.Rename); err != nil {
            log.Fatal(err)
        }
```

```
        defer notify.Stop(c)
        ei := <-c
        log.Println("Got event:", ei)
    }
}
```

gosx-notifier

This last package is for Mac users. Ever wanted to create a notification on your macOS Desktop? The `gosx-notifier` package allows you to send and display notifications through the built-in notification center.

Installation

```
$ go get github.com/deckarep/gosx-notifier
```

Code sample

```
package main

import (
    "log"

    gosxnotifier "github.com/deckarep/gosx-notifier"
)

func main() {
    note := gosxnotifier.NewNotification("Meeting with the
    team")
    note.Title = "Meeting"
    note.Subtitle = "Project discussion"
    note.Sound = gosxnotifier.Basso
    note.Group = "com.unique.yourapp.identifier"
    note.Sender = "com.apple.Safari"
    note.AppIcon = "gopher.png"
    note.ContentImage = "gopher.png"
    if err := note.Push(); err != nil {
        log.Println(err)
    }
}
```

Chapter **19**

Ten Great Go Resources

I hope this book covers all the important concepts you need to know to succeed in Go programming, but I know you need more than just one single resource to stay ahead. In this chapter, I provide ten great Go resources that will be useful to you when you're ready to venture beyond the basics.

The Official Go Website

On the official website for the Go programming language (`https://golang.org`), you can do the following:

» Download and install Go on your machine.

» Try the Go playground.

» View the documentation and tutorials for Go.

» View the documentation for the list of packages shipped with Go.

» Read the Go blog.

Go by Example

Go by Example (`https://gobyexample.com`) is a hands-on introduction to Go programming. Each example is a stand-alone program that illustrates a specific topic. The various statements in the examples are heavily annotated, making this site a very good resource for beginners.

When I was getting started with Go, I found Go by Example to be a helpful resource.

A Tour of Go

A Tour of Go (`https://tour.golang.org/`) is an interactive tutorial where you can learn, read, and write Go code directly in your web browser. One very cool feature of A Tour of Go is that it supports offline mode as well (`https://tour.golang.org/welcome/3`). After you've installed Go and A Tour of Go locally on your machine, you can view this tutorial even when you're offline. Now you have no more excuses for not learning Go, even when you're hiking in the mountains!

The Go Frequently Asked Questions

Need to know why certain features in Go were designed the way they were? Why doesn't Go support the ternary operator? How is Google using Go internally? The Golang FAQ (`https://golang.org/doc/faq`) is maintained by the Go team and is a good read when you have a burning question on Go and its design philosophy.

The Go Playground

Need to share Go code with your coworkers? Teaching a course in Go and need to give your students a block of Go code? Why not use the Go Playground (`https://play.golang.org`)? You can paste your Go code into the Go Playground and share the link with whoever you want. Best of all, you can run and test your Go code directly in the Go Playground!

Go Bootcamp

Go Bootcamp (`http://www.golangbootcamp.com/book/`) is a companion book to the Go Bootcamp event organized for the first time in Santa Monica, California, in March 2014. It's an online Go book organized into 12 chapters. If you need to read up on the syntax of Go in more detail, this is a good free resource.

Effective Go

Effective Go (`https://golang.org/doc/effective_go.html`) provides tips for writing clear, idiomatic Go code. After you're clear on the fundamentals of the Go language, head over here to learn how to write good Go code and follow established conventions for programming in Go.

Gophercises

Gophercises (`https://gophercises.com`) is a free course composed of mini-exercises to help Go developers practice writing Go programs and, in the process, gain experience with the language. In this course, you build about 20 applications, making use of the various concepts covered in *Go Programming Language For Dummies* — channels, mutexes, goroutines, functions, and so on.

Tutorialspoint

Tutorialspoint is a website dedicated to providing online education in a variety of fields. It's a popular site for learning programming languages such as JavaScript, Python, and more. So, it's no surprise that Tutorialspoint also has a section on Go programming (`www.tutorialspoint.com/go`). The next time you need a quick refresher on some Go concepts, head over to Tutorialspoint.

Stack Overflow

No resource list would be complete if it didn't mention Stack Overflow, a question-and-answer site for professional and enthusiast programmers. In fact, if you don't know Stack Overflow, you aren't a programmer yet!

It's a great place to get answers to your questions on Go (`https://stackoverflow.com/questions/tagged/go`). In fact, if you search the web for the answer to your question, chances are, Stack Overflow already has what you're looking for!

Index

Symbols

&& operator, 40

_ (blank identifier), 28, 71

`` (back ticks), 29

, (comma), 131

 (curly braces), 130

: (colon), 46, 93

// (double-slash), 24

-- operator, 53

. . . (ellipses), 72

! operator, 40

== (equal to) operator, 38

> (greater than) operator, 38, 39

>= (greater than or equal to) operator, 38, 39

< (less than) operator, 38, 39

<= (less than or equal to) operator, 38, 39

% (modulo) operator, 38

!= (not equal to) operator, 38, 39

++ operator, 53

|| operator, 40

:= (short variable declaration operator), 26–27, 39

? (ternary operator), 45

_ (underscore character), 277

A

adding
  methods to types, 158
  records, 280–281

AddInt64() function, 173–174

addNums() function, 71, 72

aggregate data type, 23

Amazon, 225–226

anonymous functions
  declaring, 73–74
  implementing closure using, 74–76
  implementing filter() function using closure, 76–78

APIs, REST
  about, 243
  building web services using, 243–248
  creating in Go, 249–269
  getting up and running, 249–251
  HTTP messages, 244
  passing in query string, 254–255
  registering additional paths, 251–254
  REST methods, 246–247
  REST response, 248
  REST URLs, 244–246
  specifying request methods, 255–257
  storing course information on, 257–267
  testing, 251, 267–269

APIs, web
  about, 225–226
  decoding JSON data, 229–233
  fetching data from web services, 226–241
  fetching from multiple web services, 238–239
  refactoring code for decoding JSON data, 233–238
  returning Goroutine's results to main() function, 239–241
  writing Go programs to connect to, 227–229

append() function, 88, 97–98

appending, to slices, 88–91

Area() function, 155–157, 158, 162

arguments. *see* parameters

array literal, 83, 88

Array value, 132–133

arrays
  about, 81–82, 92
  copying, 95–97
  declaring, 82–83
  decoding JSON to, 136–137
  extracting parts of, 92–94
  initializing, 83
  iterating through, 56–57
  multidimensional, 83–86

Atoi() function, 33

atomic counters, modifying shared resources with, 172–174

atomic package, 172

attribute names, mapping custom, 140–141

B

back ticks (``), 29

basic data type, 23

bin directory, 222

blank identifier (_), 28, 71

Boolean value, 131

break statement, 59, 62

buffered channels, 192–193

build command, 16, 19

building

   courses, 258–260

   databases, 274–275

   empty slices, 86–88

   maps, 113–121

   maps of structs, 121–123

   modules, 211–214, 214–216

   new accounts, 275–276

   REST APIs in Go, 249–269

   shareable packages, 200–202

   slices, 88

   structs, 104–105

   tables, 274–275

   web services using REST APIs, 243–248

C

C# language, 104

cap field, 87

cap() function, 87

channels

   about, 179–180

   asynchronously waiting on, 187–191

   buffered, 192–193

   how they work, 180–183

   how they're used, 183–186

   iterating through, 186–187

Cheat Sheet (website), 3

Circle struct, 155, 158, 160–161, 162

Circumference() function, 158

close() function, 187

closure

   implementing filter() function using, 76–78

   implementing filter() using, 76–78

   implementing using anonymous, 74–76

   implementing using anonymous functions, 74–76

cloud services, 8

cmp package, 110–111

Coding with JavaScript For Dummies (Minnick and Holland), 130

colon (:), 46, 93

color package, 287–288

comma (,), 131

Command Prompt window, 11

command-line apps, 9

communicating, between Goroutines using channels. *see* channels

comparing structs, 110–112

comparison operators, 38–40

compiling

   Go compared with other languages, 22

   for multiple operating systems, 19–21

   programs, 15–16

concurrent programming

   defined, 165

   Go compared with other languages, 22

condition expression, 52

connecting to MySQL databases, 276–284

const keyword, 27

constants, declaring, 27

constructor function, 104

continue statement, 59, 62–63

converting variable type, 32–34

coordinate package, finding documentation for, 208–209

copy() function, 96

copying

   arrays, 95–97

   slices, 95–97

   structs, 105–107

counter() function, 188, 189
CountOddEven() method, 152–154
course() function, 256, 258–260, 260–262
creating
  courses, 258–260
  databases, 274–275
  empty slices, 86–88
  maps, 113–121
  maps of structs, 121–123
  modules, 211–214, 214–216
  new accounts, 275–276
  REST APIs in Go, 249–269
  shareable packages, 200–202
  slices, 88
  structs, 104–105
  tables, 274–275
  web services using REST APIs, 243–248
credit() function, 168–170, 174
critical section, 172
curl command, 256–257
curly braces (), 130
Customer struct, 145–146

D

data
  decoding (see JavaScript Object Notation (JSON))
  encoding (see JavaScript Object Notation (JSON))
  fetching from web services, 226–241
data types
  about, 23
  declaring constants, 27
  declaring variables, 24–27
  performing type conversions, 30–35
  removing variables, 27–28
  specifying, 25
  strings, 29–30
databases
  about, 271
  adding records, 280–281
  connecting to MySQL database, 276–284
  creating, 274–275

creating new accounts, 275–276
creating tables and, 274–275
deleting records, 283–284
granting permission, 275–276
interfacing with MySQL server, 272–274
modifying records, 281–282
retrieving records, 278–280
setting up MySQL database server, 272–276
date formatting, 67
debit() function, 168–170, 174
decision-making
  about, 37
  if/else statement, 37–45
  switch statement, 46–49
declaring
  anonymous, 73–74
  anonymous functions, 73–74
  arrays, 82–83
  constants, 27
  variables, 24–27
decoding
  data (see JavaScript Object Notation (JSON))
  embedded objects, 137–139
  JSON, 134–144
  JSON data, 229–233
  JSON to arrays, 136–137
  JSON to structs, 135–136
defining
  functions, 65–73
  interfaces, 152–153
  method signatures (see interfaces)
  methods in structs, 107–109
  structs for collections of items, 101–103
delete() function, 99–100, 116
DELETE method, 263–267
DeleteRecord() function, 283–284
deleting
  courses, 263–267
  keys, 116
  records, 283–284
details key, 138
DigitsCounter interface, 152, 153–154

DigitString interface, 153–154

directories, organizing packages using, 202–204

displayDate() function, 66, 67–68

displayTime() function, 18

double-slash (//), 24

downloading Visual Studio Code, 12

E

EditRecord() function, 281–282

Effective Go, 301

ellipses (...), 72

else statement, 41–42

embedded objects, decoding, 137–139

emojis, for Go, 204–205

empty interfaces, 161

Encode() function, 257–258

encoding

  data (see JavaScript Object Notation (JSON))

  interfaces to JSON, 148–150

  JSON, 144–150

  structs to JSON, 144–148

env command, 19–20

environment variables, for operating systems, 20

Equal() method, 112

equal to (==) operator, 38

evaluating conditions, 42–43

Exec() function, 280–281, 282, 283–284

extracting parts of arrays/slices, 92–94

F

fallthrough keyword, 47–48

fetchData() function, 233–234, 238

fetching

  data from web services, 226–241

  from multiple web services, 238–239

fib() function, 75–76, 186–187, 188, 189

Fibonacci sequence, 54, 75–76, 186–187

fields, 102

file command, 21

file structure (Go), 18–19

filter() function, 76–78

Fixer, 227

float32() function, 34

float64() function, 34

floating-point number, 131

for loop, 59–63, 189, 191

for statement, performing loops using, 51–56

for-range loop, 57, 58, 95, 117, 118, 123, 232

Fprintf() function, 251

func keyword, 65

functions

  about, 65

  AddInt64(), 173–174

  addNums(), 71, 72

  anonymous, 73–78

  append(), 88, 97–98

  Area(), 155–157, 158, 162

  Atoi(), 33

  cap(), 87

  Circumference(), 158

  close(), 187

  constructor, 104

  copy(), 96

  counter(), 188, 189

  course(), 256, 258–262

  credit(), 168–170, 174

  debit(), 168–170, 174

  defining, 65–73

  delete(), 99–100, 116

  DeleteRecord(), 283–284

  displayDate(), 66, 67–68

  displayTime(), 18

  EditRecord(), 281–282

  Encode(), 257–258

  Exec(), 280–281, 282, 283–284

  fetchData(), 233–234, 238

  fib(), 75–76, 186–187, 188, 189

  filter(), 76–78

  float32(), 34

  float64(), 34

  Fprintf(), 251

  gen(), 76

  Get(), 226–227

getData(), 180–183
home(), 250
insert(), 97–98
InsertRecord(), 280–281
int(), 34
json.Marshal(), 146, 148–150
json.Unmarshal(), 135–136, 142
Kind(), 31
LastInsertId(), 280–281
len(), 30, 83, 87, 116–117, 120
length(), 107–109, 198–199, 200, 202
less(), 120
Lock(), 172, 174
main(), 17, 69, 70, 166–167, 174, 181, 187, 191, 197–198, 235, 239–241, 258–260, 277, 283–284
make(), 86, 87, 114, 115, 181, 187, 192
map(), 76
Marshal(), 146
MarshalIndent(), 147
Methods(), 255–256
move(), 109
mux.Vars(), 252
newPoint(), 104, 105
Next(), 279
Parse, 33–34
Printf(), 58–59
Println(), 17, 24, 29, 31, 72, 159–160
Query(), 279
raining(), 43
randSeed(), 183
ReadAll(), 227
reduce(), 76
returning values from, 71
RowsAffected(), 280–281, 282, 283–284
RuneCountInString(), 30
r.URL.Query(), 254–255
say(), 166–167
Scan(), 279
Scanf(), 32–33
Scanln(), 167, 174, 239
sendData(), 180–183
Slice(), 126–127

SliceStable(), 124–127
snowing(), 43
sort(), 120
Sprintf(), 35
sql.Open(), 277–278
String(), 160–161
sum(), 183–184, 193
swap(), 68–69, 70, 120
TypeOf(), 31
Unlock(), 172, 174
ValueOf(), 31
variadic, 72–73, 98
Vars(), 252
Wait(), 175
wg.–176Add(), 175
wg.Done(), 175–176
wg.Wait(), 175–176

G

garbage collection (GC), 22
GCP. see Google Cloud Platform (GCP)
gen() function, 76
generating
    courses, 258–260
    databases, 274–275
    empty slices, 86–88
    maps, 113–121
    maps of structs, 121–123
    modules, 211–214, 214–216
    new accounts, 275–276
    REST APIs in Go, 249–269
    shareable packages, 200–202
    slices, 88
    structs, 104–105
    tables, 274–275
    web services using REST APIs, 243–248
generics, 8
Get() function, 226–227
GET method, 246–247, 262
getData() function, 180–183
GitHub, publishing modules on, 216–222

Go. *see also specific topics*
  about, 7
  advantages of learning, 8–9
  Bootcamp, 301
  compared with other languages, 21–22
  creating REST APIs in, 249–269
  emojis for, 204–205
  evaluating conditions in, 42–43
  FAQ, 300
  file structure, 18–19
  how programs work, 17
  installer, 10
  installing, 9–11
  Playground, 300
  using integrated development environment (IDE) with, 12–14
  versions, 10
  website, 7, 9, 299
  writing your first program, 14–21
"Go at Google Language Design in the Service of Software Engineering," 7
Go by Example, 300
Go Documentation (Godoc), 205–207
go env command, 201
Go extension, installing for Visual Studio Code, 12–14
go install command, 203
go keyword, 167
go run command, 202
go-http-client package, 295–296
goid package, 290–291
gojq package, 292–294
GoLand, 12
Golang. *see* Go
Google Cloud Platform (GCP), 8
Google Finance, 226
$GOPATH, subdirectories within, 222
GOPATH environment variable, 201, 203
Gophercises, 301
go-pushbullet package, 289–290

gorilla/mux package, 249
Goroutines
  about, 165–167
  communicating between using channels (*see* channels)
  returning results to main(), 239–241
  returning results to main() function, 239–241
  synchronizing, 174–178
  using with shared resources, 168–174
gosx-notifier package, 297
The Go Playground, 12
granting permission, 275–276
greater than (>) operator, 38, 39
greater than or equal to (>=) operator, 38, 39
Griesemer, Robert (engineer), 7
grouping packages. *see* modules

H

half-open range, 92–93
Holland, Eva (author)
  Coding with JavaScript For Dummies, 130
home() function, 250
HTTP messages, 244

I

icons, explained, 2–3
IDE (integrated development environment), using with Go, 12–14
idiomatic, 104
if statement, 41–42
if/else statements
  about, 37
  comparison operators, 38–40
  logical operators, 38–40
  using, 40–42
implementing
  closure using anonymous, 74–76
  closure using anonymous functions, 74–76
  filter() function using closure, 76–78

filter() using closure, 76–78
  interfaces, 153–154
  multiple interfaces, 160–161
infinite loops, 55–56
inheritance, 8
init statement, 52
initialization statement, 44
initializing
  arrays, 83
  maps with map literals, 115
  slices, 88
insert() function, 97–98
inserting items to slices, 97–99
InsertRecord() function, 280–281
installing
  Go, 9–11
  Go extension for Visual Studio Code, 12–14
int() function, 34
int key, 122
integer, 131
integrated development environment (IDE), using
    with Go, 12–14
interface data type, 23
interfaces
  about, 151
  defining, 152–153
  empty, 161
  encoding to JSON, 148–150
  implementing, 153–154
  implementing multiple, 160–161
  with MySQL server, 272–274
  using, 154–162
  values and, 162
  working with, 152–154
Internet resources
  Amazon, 225–226
  Cheat Sheet, 3
  Effective Go, 301
  Fixer, 227

Go, 7, 9, 299
"Go at Google Language Design in the
    Service of Software Engineering," 7
Go Bootcamp, 301
Go by Example, 300
Go FAQ, 300
Go Playground, 300
GoLand, 12
Google Finance, 226
Gophercises, 301
The Go Playground, 12
JSON strings, 134
JSONLint, 235
MySQL database server, 272
MySQL Workbench, 272
npm, 204
OpenWeather, 235
PyPI, 204
Stack Overflow, 302
Stack Overflow Developer
    Survey, 8
A Tour of Go, 300
Tutorialspoint, 301
Visual Studio Code, 12
XML, 129
interpolating strings, 34–35
iterating
  over maps, 117
  over ranges of values, 56–59
  setting order for, in maps, 118
  through arrays/slices, 56–57
  through channels, 186–187
  through slices, 95
  through strings, 58–59

J

Java, 21–22
Java language, 104

JavaScript Object Notation (JSON)
about, 129–130
Array value, 132–133
Boolean value, 131
decoding, 134–144
decoding data, 229–233
decoding embedded objects, 137–139
decoding to arrays, 136–137
decoding to structs, 135–136
encoding, 144–150
encoding interfaces to, 148–150
encoding structs to, 144–148
mapping custom attribute names, 140–141
mapping unstructured data, 141–144
null value, 133–134
Number value, 131
Object value, 130, 132
String value, 130–131
json2go package, 291–292
JSONLint, 235
json.Marshal() function, 146, 148–150
json.Unmarshal() function, 135–136, 142

K

keys
checking existence of, 115–116
defined, 113
deleting, 116
getting in maps, 117
key-value pairs, 130–131
Kind() function, 31

L

labels, using with for loop, 59–63
LastInsertId() function, 280–281
len field, 87
len() function, 30, 83, 87, 116–117, 120
length() function, 107–109, 198–199, 200, 202
less() function, 120
less than (>) operator, 38, 39
less than or equal to (<=) operator, 38, 39

library support, Go compared with other languages, 22
Lock() function, 172, 174
logical operators, 38–40
loops
-- operator, 53
++ operator, 53
about, 51
infinite, 55–56
iterating over ranges of values, 56–59
iterating through arrays/slices, 56–57
iterating through strings, 58–59
performing using for statement, 51–56
using labels with for loop, 59–63

M

macOS
downloading MySQL database server, 272
Go Documentation (Godoc), 206–207
installing Go, 10–11
main() function, 17, 69, 70, 166–167, 174, 181, 187, 191, 197–198, 235, 239–241, 258–260, 277, 283–284
make() function, 86, 87, 114, 115, 181, 187, 192
map() function, 76
map literals, initializing maps with, 115
mapping
custom attribute names, 140–141
unstructured data, 141–144
maps
about, 113
checking existence of keys, 115–116
creating, 113–121
creating of structs, 121–123
deleting keys, 116
getting keys in, 117
getting number of items in, 116–117
initializing with map literals, 115
iterating over, 117
setting iteration order in, 118
sorting items by values in, 118–121
sorting of structs, 124–127
structs and, 121–127

Marshal() function, 146
MarshalIndent() function, 147
matching multiple cases, 48
method signatures, defining. *see* interfaces
methods
    adding to types, 158
    defining in structs, 107–109
    REST, 246–247
Methods() function, 255–256
Minnick, Chris (author)
    Coding with JavaScript For Dummies, 130
modifying
    records, 281–282
    shared resources with atomic counters, 172–174
modules
    about, 211
    building, 214–216
    creating, 211–214
    publishing on GitHub, 216–222
    testing, 214–216
modulo (%) operator, 38
move() function, 109
multidimensional arrays, 83–86
Mutex object, 171, 172, 174
mutual exclusion, accessing shared resources
    using, 171–172
mux.Vars() function, 252
MySQL database server
    interfacing with, 272–274
    setting up, 272–276
MySQL databases, connecting to, 276–284
MySQL Workbench, 272

N

naming return values, 72
networking apps, 9
newPoint() function, 104, 105
Next() function, 279
not equal to (!=) operator, 38, 39
notify package, 296–297
now package, 288–289
npm, 204
null value, 133–134

Number value, 131
nums array, 82

O

Object value, 130, 132
object-oriented programming (OOP), 8
OpenWeather, 235
operating systems
    compiling for multiple, 19–21
    environment variables for, 20

P

packages
    about, 197
    atomic, 172
    cmp, 110–111
    color, 287–288
    coordinate, 208–209
    creating shareable,
        200–202
    emojis for Go, 204–205
    finding documentation for coordinate
        package, 208–209
    Go documentation, 205–209
    go-http-client, 295–296
    goid, 290–291
    gojq, 292–294
    go-pushbullet, 289–290
    gorilla/mux, 249
    gosx-notifier, 297
    grouping (*see* modules)
    json2go, 291–292
    notify, 296–297
    now, 288–289
    organizing using directories,
        202–204
    recommended, 287–297
    reflect, 31
    sort, 118, 124, 233
    sync, 171
    third-party, 204–209
    turtle, 294–295
    working with, 197–204

parameterized SQL statement, 280
parameters
  defining functions with, 66–68
  defining functions with multiple, 68
  passing by value and pointer, 68–70
Parse function, 33–34
passing
  parameters by value and pointer, 68–70
  in query string, 254–255
passing by reference, 70
performing
  loops using for statement, 51–56
  type conversions, 30–35
permission, granting, 275–276
Pike, Rob (designer), 7
pkg directory, 222
point struct, 104–108, 110
pointer, passing parameters by, 68–70
pointer receiver, 109
POST method, 246–247, 260
post statement, 52
primitive types, 124
Printf() function, 58–59
Println() function, 17, 24, 29, 31, 72, 159–160
programs
  compiling, 15–16
  running, 15–16
properties, 8
ptr field, 87
publishing modules, on GitHub, 216–222
PUT method, 246–247, 260
PyPI, 204
Python, 21–22

Q

Query() function, 279
query strings, passing in, 254–255

R

raining() function, 43
randSeed() function, 183

range keyword, 57, 186–187
ReadAll() function, 227
receiver, 107
records
  adding, 280–281
  deleting, 283–284
  modifying, 281–282
  retrieving, 278–280
reduce() function, 76
refactoring code, for decoding JSON data, 233–238
reference, passing by, 70
reference data type, 23
reflect package, 31
registering additional paths, 251–254
Remember icon, 2
removing
  items from slices, 99–100
  variables, 27–28
representational state transfer (REST). *see* REST APIs
request methods, specifying, 255–257
resources, Internet
  Amazon, 225–226
  Cheat Sheet, 3
  Effective Go, 301
  Fixer, 227
  Go, 7, 9, 299
  "Go at Google Language Design in the Service of Software Engineering," 7
  Go Bootcamp, 301
  Go by Example, 300
  Go FAQ, 300
  Go Playground, 300
  GoLand, 12
  Google Finance, 226
  Gophercises, 301
  The Go Playground, 12
  JSON strings, 134
  JSONLint, 235
  MySQL database server, 272
  MySQL Workbench, 272
  npm, 204

OpenWeather, 235
PyPI, 204
Stack Overflow, 302
Stack Overflow Developer Survey, 8
A Tour of Go, 300
Tutorialspoint, 301
Visual Studio Code, 12
XML, 129
resources, recommended, 299–302
resources, shared
  accessing using mutual exclusion, 171–172
  modifying with atomic counters, 172–174
  using Goroutines with, 168–174
REST APIs
  about, 243
  building web services using, 243–248
  creating in Go, 249–269
  getting up and running, 249–251
  HTTP messages, 244
  passing in query string, 254–255
  registering additional paths, 251–254
  REST methods, 246–247
  REST response, 248
  REST URLs, 244–246
  specifying request methods, 255–257
  storing course information on, 257–267
  testing, 251, 267–269
REST methods, 246–247
REST response, 248
REST URLs, 244–246
retrieving
  courses, 262
  records, 278–280
return statement, 72, 191
return values, naming, 72
returning
  Goroutine's results to main( ), 239–241
  Goroutine's results to main( ) function, 239–241
  values from functions, 71
RowsAffected( ) function, 280–281, 282, 283–284
RuneCountInString( ) function, 30
running programs, 15–16
r.URL.Query( ) function, 254–255

S

say( ) function, 166–167
Scan( ) function, 279
Scanf( ) function, 32–33
Scanln( ) function, 167, 174, 239
select statement, 189
sendData( ) function, 180–183
Shape interface, 155, 157, 158, 162
shared resources
  accessing using mutual exclusion, 171–172
  modifying with atomic counters, 172–174
  using Goroutines with, 168–174
short variable declaration operator (:=), 26–27, 39
Slice( ) function, 126–127
slice header, 87
slices
  about, 86, 92
  appending to, 88–91
  copying, 95–97
  creating, 88
  creating empty, 86–88
  extracting parts of, 92–94
  initializing, 88
  inserting items to, 97–99
  iterating through, 56–57, 95
  removing items from, 99–100
SliceStable( ) function, 124–127
snowing( ) function, 43
sort( ) function, 120
sort package, 118, 124, 233
sorting
  items by values in maps, 118–121
  maps of structs, 124–127
specifying
  data types, 25
  request methods, 255–257
Sprintf( ) function, 35
sql.Open( ) function, 277–278
Square struct, 155
src directory, 222
Stack Overflow, 302
Stack Overflow Developer Survey, 8

storing course information, on REST API, 257–267

String() function, 160–161

String value, 130–131

Stringer interface, 159–160, 160–161

strings

  interpolating, 34–35

  iterating through, 58–59

  managing, 29–30

struct field tags, 140

structs

  about, 101

  Circle, 155, 158, 160–161, 162

  comparing, 110–112

  copying, 105–107

  creating, 104–105

  creating maps of, 121–123

  Customer, 145–146

  decoding JSON to, 135–136

  defining for collections of items, 101–103

  defining methods in, 107–109

  encoding to JSON, 144–148

  maps and, 121–127

  point, 104–108, 110

  sorting maps of, 124–127

  Square, 155

  Triangle, 157

structured types, 124

subdirectories, within $GOPATH, 222

sum() function, 183–184, 193

swap() function, 68–69, 70, 120

switch statement

  about, 46–47

  fallthrough keyword, 47–48

  matching multiple cases, 48

  without condition, 48–49

sync package, 171

synchronizing Goroutines, 174–178

syntax, Go compared with other languages, 21–22

T

%T, 31

tables, creating, 274–275

Technical Stuff icon, 2

Terminal app, 10–11

ternary operator (?), 45

testing

  modules, 214–216

  REST APIs, 251, 267–269

third-party packages

  about, 204

  emojis for Go, 204–205

  finding documentation for coordinate package, 208–209

  Go documentation, 205–209

Thompson, Ken (designer), 7

threading. *see* Goroutines

three-dimensional (3D) coordinate space, 102

time formatting, 67

Tip icon, 3

A Tour of Go, 300

Triangle struct, 157

turtle package, 294–295

Tutorialspoint, 301

two-dimensional (2D) coordinate space, 101–102

TypeOf() function, 31

types

  adding methods to, 158

  performing conversions, 30–35

U

underscore character (_), 277

Unicode characters, 30, 58

Unlock() function, 172, 174

unstructured data, mapping, 141–144

updating courses, 260–262

V

value receiver, 108

ValueOf() function, 31

values

  interfaces and, 162

  iterating over ranges of, 56–59

  passing parameters by, 68–70

  return, 72

returning from functions, 71

sorting items by, in maps, 118–121

var keyword, 24–25, 102

variables

converting type, 32–34

declaring, 24–27

removing, 27–28

types of, 31

variadic functions, 72–73, 98

Vars( ) function, 252

versions (Go), 10

Visual Studio Code

about, 12

downloading, 12

installing Go extension for, 12–14

W

Wait( ) function, 175

wait group, 175

Warning icon, 3

web APIs

about, 225–226

decoding JSON data, 229–233

fetching data from web services, 226–241

fetching from multiple web services, 238–239

refactoring code for decoding JSON data, 233–238

returning Goroutine's results to main( ) function, 239–241

writing Go programs to connect to, 227–229

web services

building using REST APIs, 243–248

using Go on, 9

websites

Amazon, 225–226

Cheat Sheet, 3

Effective Go, 301

Fixer, 227

Go, 7, 9, 299

"Go at Google Language Design in the Service of Software Engineering," 7

Go Bootcamp, 301

Go by Example, 300

Go FAQ, 300

Go Playground, 300

GoLand, 12

Google Finance, 226

Gophercises, 301

The Go Playground, 12

JSON strings, 134

JSONLint, 235

MySQL database server, 272

MySQL Workbench, 272

npm, 204

OpenWeather, 235

PyPI, 204

Stack Overflow, 302

Stack Overflow Developer Survey, 8

A Tour of Go, 300

Tutorialspoint, 301

Visual Studio Code, 12

XML, 129

wg.–176Add( ) function, 175

wg.Done( ) function, 175–176

wg.Wait( ) function, 175–176

Windows

downloading MySQL database server, 272

Go Documentation (Godoc), 206

installing Go, 11

writing

Go programs, 14–21

Go programs to connect to web APIs, 227–229

X

x coordinate, 101–102

XML, 129

Y

y coordinate, 101–102

About the Author

Wei-Meng Lee is a technologist and founder of Developer Learning Solutions (http://calendar.learn2develop.net), a company specializing in hands-on training on the latest technologies.

Wei-Meng has many years of training experience. His training courses place special emphasis on the learning-by-doing approach. Wei-Meng's hands-on approach to learning programming makes understanding the subject much easier than reading books, tutorials, and documentation. His name regularly appears in online and print publications, such as DevX.com, MobiForge.com, and *CODE Magazine*. He is also the author of *Python Machine Learning* (Wiley), *Learning WatchKit Programming* (Addison-Wesley), *Beginning Swift Programming* (Wrox), and *SwiftUI For Dummies* (Wiley).

When he's not coding, Wei-Meng speaks at meetups and conferences, such as NDC Oslo, NDC London, NDC Copenhagen, and RigaDevDays.

Dedication

I dedicate this book with love to my dearest wife, Sze Wa, and daughter, Chloe, who have to endure my irregular work schedule and for their companionship when I'm trying to meet writing deadlines!

Author's Acknowledgments

Writing a book is always exciting, but along with it come long hours of hard work, straining to get things done accurately and correctly. To make a book possible, many unsung heroes work tirelessly behind the scenes. I would like to take this opportunity to thank a number of special people who have made this book possible.

First, I want to thank Executive Editor Steven Hayes, for his trust in me to write my second *For Dummies* book. It has been a great working experience dealing with the Dummies team, and I'm proud to be a Dummies author! Thank you, Steve!

Next, a huge thanks to Elizabeth Kuball, my project editor, who is always a pleasure to work with. I was super excited when I heard that Elizabeth was going to be my editor for my second *For Dummies* book! With Elizabeth onboard, I know the project is in good hands! Give me a high-five, Elizabeth! (And thanks for the patience when I occasionally missed the deadlines.)

Equally important is my technical editor, Chaim Krause. I've known Chaim for close to a decade, and I've worked with him on several book projects. Chaim can always be relied upon to spot my mistakes, and his technical-editing skills certainly made this book a better one. Thanks, Chaim!

I also want to specially thank Patrice Choong, Director of the School of InfoComm Technology, Ngee Ann Polytechnic, for giving me the opportunity to get involved with the curriculum development at The Go School and The Data School, and for his trust in me. Thank you, Patrice!

Last, but not least, I want to thank my parents, my wife, and my lovely girl, for all the support they've given me. They selflessly adjusted their schedules to accommodate my busy schedule when I was working on this book. I love you all!

Publisher's Acknowledgments

Executive Editor: Steven Hayes

Project Editor: Elizabeth Kuball

Copy Editor: Elizabeth Kuball

Technical Editor: Chaim Krause

Production Editor: Tamilmani Varadharaj

Cover Image: © JoffBarnes/E+/Getty Images

Take dummies with you everywhere you go!

Whether you are excited about e-books, want more from the web, must have your mobile apps, or are swept up in social media, dummies makes everything easier.

Find us online!

Leverage the power

Dummies is the global leader in the reference category and one of the most trusted and highly regarded brands in the world. No longer just focused on books, customers now have access to the dummies content they need in the format they want. Together we'll craft a solution that engages your customers, stands out from the competition, and helps you meet your goals.

Advertising & Sponsorships

Connect with an engaged audience on a powerful multimedia site, and position your message alongside expert how-to content. Dummies.com is a one-stop shop for free, online information and know-how curated by a team of experts.

- Targeted ads
- Video
- Email Marketing
- Microsites
- Sweepstakes sponsorship

20 MILLION PAGE VIEWS EVERY SINGLE MONTH

15 MILLION UNIQUE VISITORS PER MONTH

43% OF ALL VISITORS ACCESS THE SITE VIA THEIR MOBILE DEVICES

700,000 NEWSLETTER SUBSCRIPTIONS TO THE INBOXES OF *300,000* UNIQUE INDIVIDUALS EVERY WEEK

# of dummies

Custom Publishing

Reach a global audience in any language by creating a solution that will differentiate you from competitors, amplify your message, and encourage customers to make a buying decision.

- Apps
- Books
- eBooks
- Video
- Audio
- Webinars

Brand Licensing & Content

Leverage the strength of the world's most popular reference brand to reach new audiences and channels of distribution.

For more information, visit **dummies.com/biz**

PERSONAL ENRICHMENT

 **Staying Sharp**
9781119187790
USA $26.00
CAN $31.99
UK £19.99

 **Facebook**
Carolyn Abram
9781119179030
USA $21.99
CAN $25.99
UK £16.99

 **Guitar**
Mark Phillips
Jon Chappell
9781119293354
USA $24.99
CAN $29.99
UK £17.99

 **Investing**
Eric Tyson, MBA
9781119293347
USA $22.99
CAN $27.99
UK £16.99

 **Beekeeping**
Howland Blackiston
9781119310068
USA $22.99
CAN $27.99
UK £16.99

 **Digital Photography**
Julie Adair King
9781119235606
USA $24.99
CAN $29.99
UK £17.99

 **Meditation**
Stephan Bodian
9781119251163
USA $24.99
CAN $29.99
UK £17.99

 **Pregnancy**
9781119235491
USA $26.99
CAN $31.99
UK £19.99

 **Samsung Galaxy S7**
Bill Hughes
9781119279952
USA $24.99
CAN $29.99
UK £17.99

 iPhone
Edward C. Baig
Bob "Dr. Mac" LeVitus
9781119283133
USA $24.99
CAN $29.99
UK £17.99

 **Crocheting**
Karen Manthey
Susan Brittain
9781119287117
USA $24.99
CAN $29.99
UK £16.99

 **Nutrition**
Carol Ann Rinzler
9781119130246
USA $22.99
CAN $27.99
UK £16.99

PROFESSIONAL DEVELOPMENT

 **Windows 10**
Andy Rathbone
9781119311041
USA $24.99
CAN $29.99
UK £17.99

 **AutoCAD**
Bill Fane
9781119255796
USA $39.99
CAN $47.99
UK £27.99

 **Excel 2016**
Greg Harvey, PhD
9781119293439
USA $26.99
CAN $31.99
UK £19.99

 **QuickBooks 2017**
Stephen L. Nelson, MBA, CPA, MS in Taxation
9781119281467
USA $26.99
CAN $31.99
UK £19.99

 **macOS Sierra**
Bob "Dr. Mac" LeVitus
9781119280651
USA $29.99
CAN $35.99
UK £21.99

 **LinkedIn**
Joel Elad, MBAs
9781119251132
USA $24.99
CAN $29.99
UK £17.99

 **Windows 10**
Woody Leonhard
9781119310563
USA $34.00
CAN $41.99
UK £24.99

 **SharePoint 2016**
Rosemarie Withee
Ken Withee
9781119181705
USA $29.99
CAN $35.99
UK £21.99

 **Fundamental Analysis**
Matt Krantz
9781119263593
USA $26.99
CAN $31.99
UK £19.99

 **Networking**
Doug Lowe
9781119257769
USA $29.99
CAN $35.99
UK £21.99

 **Office 2016**
Wallace Wang
9781119293477
USA $26.99
CAN $31.99
UK £19.99

 **Office 365**
Rosemarie Withee
Ken Withee
Jennifer Reed
9781119265313
USA $24.99
CAN $29.99
UK £17.99

 **Salesforce.com**
Liz Kao
Jon Paz
9781119239314
USA $29.99
CAN $35.99
UK £21.99

 **Coding**
Nikhil Abraham
9781119293323
USA $29.99
CAN $35.99
UK £21.99

dummies.com

dummies®
A Wiley Brand

Learning Made Easy

ACADEMIC

9781119293576
USA $19.99
CAN $23.99
UK £15.99

9781119293637
USA $19.99
CAN $23.99
UK £15.99

9781119293491
USA $19.99
CAN $23.99
UK £15.99

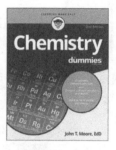

9781119293460
USA $19.99
CAN $23.99
UK £15.99

9781119293590
USA $19.99
CAN $23.99
UK £15.99

9781119215844
USA $26.99
CAN $31.99
UK £19.99

9781119293378
USA $22.99
CAN $27.99
UK £16.99

9781119293521
USA $19.99
CAN $23.99
UK £15.99

9781119239178
USA $18.99
CAN $22.99
UK £14.99

9781119263883
USA $26.99
CAN $31.99
UK £19.99

Available Everywhere Books Are Sold

dummies.com

Small books for big imaginations

9781119177173
USA $9.99
CAN $9.99
UK £8.99

9781119177272
USA $9.99
CAN $9.99
UK £8.99

9781119177241
USA $9.99
CAN $9.99
UK £8.99

9781119177210
USA $9.99
CAN $9.99
UK £8.99

9781119262657
USA $9.99
CAN $9.99
UK £6.99

9781119291336
USA $9.99
CAN $9.99
UK £6.99

9781119233527
USA $9.99
CAN $9.99
UK £6.99

9781119291220
USA $9.99
CAN $9.99
UK £6.99

9781119177302
USA $9.99
CAN $9.99
UK £8.99

Unleash Their Creativity

dummies.com